PIGEONHOLING WOMEN'S MISERY

PIGEONHOLING WOMEN'S MISERY

A HISTORY AND CRITICAL ANALYSIS OF THE PSYCHODIAGNOSIS OF WOMEN IN THE TWENTIETH CENTURY

HANNAH LERMAN, PH.D.

BasicBooks
A Division of HarperCollins*Publishers*

Copyright © 1996 by BasicBooks,
A Division of HarperCollins Publishers, Inc.

Library of Congress Cataloging-in-Publication Data

Lerman, Hannah.
   Pigeonholing women's misery : a history and critical analysis of the psychodiagnosis of women in the twentieth century / Hannah Lerman.
     p. cm.
   Includes bibliographical references and index.
   ISBN 0-465-09533-X
   1. Women—Mental health—Sociological aspects. 2. Mental illness—Diagnosis—Social aspects. 3. Mental illness—Classification—Social aspects. 4. Feminist therapy. 5. Deviant behavior—Labeling theory.   I. Title.
RC451.4.W6L465   1996
616.89'075'082—dc20   96-15760
                                                CIP

96 97 98 99 ❖/HC 9 8 7 6 5 4 3 2

For my mother, whom I did not know
and who did not know me
because of how we were taught to be.

CONTENTS

ACKNOWLEDGMENTS

WHEN I PUBLISHED my first book in 1986, the literature in feminist psychology was still in its early stages. I had read much prefeminist literature and, with some exceptions, reached my own conclusions relatively independently. For that book I was able to acknowledge directly the specific people from whom I learned, as well as those who helped me more directly.

Today this is less possible; in effect, every author whose work is cited (and many whose work I read but did not cite directly) taught me something. I also have gained immeasurably from colleagues (mostly, but not exclusively, female) to whom I listened and with whom I spoke at APA, AWP, FTI, and other meetings; this book could not have materialized without these experiences. In addition, I have learned from my clients just how hard it is for them to fit into the diagnostic pigeonholes that are available, and how badly some of them have been hurt by the overall professional efforts to fit unique, complex individuals into the *DSM* straightjacket.

I do, however, wish to indicate an intellectual debt to those people toiling in the same vineyard in which I am working and who are developing new ideas about diagnostic thinking. Hope Landrine amazed me with her ideas and, in particular, her documentation in a virtually ignored but important work on racial and gender stereotypes as they are played out in diagnosis. Since first having learned about the work of Herbert Kutchins and Stuart Kirk I have been tickled by the fact that they, doctors of social work, have exposed the truth concerning the poor reliability of the *DSM-III* and *DSM-IV*—a topic that has been sorely neglected by psychologists in whose province one would think it should have fit. Others whose thinking has a direct bearing on diagnosis in a feminist context are

Paula Caplan, Lenore Walker, and, especially, Laura Brown. I have also discussed some of my ideas (and benefited from these discussions) with Natalie Porter, Marjorie Braude, and Iris Fodor.

TDM contributed the original drawing that illustrates the aspects of diagnosis (my own drawing ability is not up to the task). She did a beautiful job and I want her to know how grateful I am for her contribution.

In terms of the actual writing of this book, I have Laura Brown to thank for nudging me to put the thoughts down on paper. I held this book extremely close to my vest and did not expose my written material to anyone without first having shown it to my editors. I wish to thank Eric Wright of Basic Books, who stepped into the breach left by my previous editors. He is understanding about my ideas and presented me with precisely the right amount of acceptance and criticism that made this a much better book.

Since the time of writing I have been tripping over additional material that I feel corroborates many of the ideas presented in these pages. Here I have tried to bring the ideas together and integrate them. Now I commend them to you, the reader, for consideration.

Hannah Lerman
June 1996

PIGEONHOLING WOMEN'S MISERY

CHAPTER 1

Diagnosis: Sense, Nonsense, and Common Sense

IN EVERYDAY LIFE, everybody "diagnoses" all the time. Anyone who takes the time to evaluate a situation or a person and then decides whether any action needs to follow from his or her assumptions about the situation could be said to have made a diagnosis. We classify, interpret, and judge the behaviors of other people based on implicit theories we hold about human behavior. Most of the time we do not even consciously realize exactly what we are doing, or even that we hold such theories about the meaning of particular behaviors we see. But our own behavior reveals that we do—or we wouldn't act. In the everyday world, nobody uses the word *diagnosis* for this process, but it typifies the most common and easily understood sense in which the term applies.

Commonly, though, we misinterpret other people's behavior, especially when their experiences differ from our own. All people get into this kind of difficulty whenever they interpret other people's behavior within the framework they use to view their own. Mistakes happen because the categories people carry in their heads have been formed out of both their own specific life experiences and what they have been explicitly taught about others. One relatively simple example is the different ways men and women interpret each other's behavior. Much research on topics such as rape and sexual harassment has demonstrated that when such touchy issues are involved, women and men react differently to identical behavior (Tavris, 1992).

In the mental health professions, the term *diagnosis* and the processes used to carry it out have a more specific and focused meaning. The professional use of the term retains the same under-

1

lying meaning as the commonsense understanding of it—that of sizing up or assessing a situation and arriving at a conclusion. It is also subject to the same problems. In theory at least, when we assess professionally, we are supposed to be conscious of the process we are undertaking and have our theoretical assumptions explicitly in mind. Obviously, this is not true as often as we claim. Despite our professional cloak, we are merely human beings with human failings. Even our theoretical perspective is not as broad and inclusive as we ideally want it to be. Quite often, despite ostensibly authoritative pronouncements, our collective professional thought processes fail to include important information about the experiences of others.

Most often, information is gathered through clinical interviews and various standardized tests. Standardized tests are the equivalent of highly structured interviews used to compare the responses of the client before us with those of other people in similar circumstances. Tests are merely tools. They suffer from the same drawbacks as interviews: Assumptions exist in the head of the interviewer, based on personal experiences, schooling, and professional experience. Just as with interviews, a test's database of responses may not come from a broad enough population and may not include persons from a background similar to the client's. Many tests are standardized upon white middle-class people, but the client to whom the norms are applied is from a different class and different ethnic and/or social background. Only recently has this problem been recognized, but in many cases, solutions to it in the form of more appropriately normed data have not been fully reached.

In every type of professional mental health context, some kind of assessment or diagnosis occurs. When a client consults a therapist in order to stop smoking, for example, the therapist will assess the nature of the person's smoking habit. The therapist usually asks the client how much he or she smokes, when he or she is most likely to smoke, and so on. The conclusions the therapist draws from the answers will help determine what kind of interventions might help the client. The professional tailors a therapy plan to the individual, built out of a diagnosis based on what he or she knows, perceives, and feels about the situation and the individual. If, however, the therapist fails to ask the appropriate questions—failing to learn, say, that the woman client never smokes in front of her mother because she fears her mother's disapproval, which she has regularly suffered since childhood—the therapist has failed to learn some important information about the context of the woman's life and the relationship of smoking to her sources of tension and difficulties with self-esteem. Depending on how much the therapist does not know about what is actually important, the therapist's interventions may fail to help the client stop smoking. Even in this relatively specific, circumscribed example, the context in which smoking is embedded for the particular client needs to be explored. As will be seen later, the failure to explore context is one of the most serious gaps in formal diagnosis, especially when diagnosis is made by someone who himself (usually) may not know much about the context in which the client lives. The appropriate knowledge, sadly, is most often missing when professional mental health workers deal with ethnic minorities and women.

The example involving smoking is a very specific one whose steps can easily be seen and understood, even when they might be overlooked. However, any therapist seeing a client for any reason or set of reasons often assesses that client intuitively (although the assessment may, as we have seen, sometimes be more overt and concrete). For example, when therapy texts refer to the timing of an intervention, they are relying on the fact that the therapist has assessed (or diagnosed, if you will) when the client is ready for that intervention.

We know that precisely what elements are considered in doing this kind of diagnosis and how its results are conveyed to the client are crucial. Laura Brown (1988) expressed the feminist view (which I hold) very well:

> I see as one of my responsibilities a formulation of hypotheses regarding the nature and sources of the distress that my clients report to me. Such formulation must follow from a coherent theory of human growth and development, and from assumptions about what factors are likely have both positive and negative impact upon that normative developmental process. For me, as a feminist, that formulation must also include an analysis of the meaning of gender and gender roles within the particular cultural context that has served as my client's milieu. Additionally, this theorizing must speak to the role of culture and cultural oppression as factors in the development of distress in human beings. Beyond giving me answers, these hypotheses must also allow me to communicate to and with my client about how I understand their problems, and do so in a way that will empower and educate them regarding the sources of distress so that they become

more fully equal partners in the work of psychotherapy. Finally, this set of hypotheses must give me guidelines about how, where and when to intervene as a therapist. They must guide my thinking regarding my role in relationship to my client, and the ways in which I apply the feminist therapy principles of egalitarian relationships, empowerment, and validation of women's diverse experiences. (p. 3)

Among the points that are significant in this view is that in addition to the person's experience of distress, the entire context in which the person lives must be considered as much as is humanly possible. Also, therapists must remain aware that their own opinions are only hypotheses, never facts, and need to be communicable to clients in the service of their own empowerment.

Diagnosis, as described to this point, is an informal and often intuitive process, even in a professional setting. Only rarely is it fully spelled out, even to the extent I have described it. Although it is a crucial part of mental health work, this informal, ongoing diagnostic process is not, however, what this book will directly focus on. Formal diagnosis as it has evolved in the mental health field refers to the process of classification and labeling to determine that an individual is suffering from a specific disorder. Ideally, however, it parallels the process of informal diagnosis. There is an implication that the diagnosis will, among other purposes, help the clinician determine appropriate treatment. We will explore some of the problems inherent in this implication later.

Just as in informal diagnosis, the process of assigning labels depends on the assessor's evaluating facts about the person being examined and then arriving at conclusions based on some set of assumptions. We know from history that professional assumptions have often been based on beliefs that do not have a factual basis and that have not considered the context of gender and other cultural factors. We also know that the assessor's conclusions are not often communicated back to the client in the service of validation and personal empowerment. Until very recently, those who formulated the system, primarily men, were often far removed from and therefore ignorant about the context and lives of the persons to whom they were assigning labels and for whom they developed classification systems.

The process of formal diagnosis has a very long history, one that is almost as long as the history of the human race itself. The ancient Greeks, for example, gave us the concept of hysteria—suffered usually by women. Originally hysteria was thought to be the result of wandering of the womb, a diagnostic assumption of the time that obviously was later proven wrong. Although the Greeks coined the word, the same concept previously existed in ancient Egypt (Veith, 1965). The issue of hysteria and related diagnoses has been a focus for women well into this century. The implications of this diagnosis based on what we now know are factually inaccurate assumptions, and its connotations (which remain), will be discussed in detail later.

The subtitle of this book indicates that it is a history and critical analysis of how the most formal diagnostic process, that of labeling, has evolved in the twentieth century, particularly as it involves women. Only in this century have the categories of the most commonly and widely used American system coalesced so that they could legitimately be called a formal classification system. This book will explore this system, how its categories have evolved and changed, and alternatives to it. Just as personal tragedies have often resulted from unrecognized bias in the informal diagnosis that everyone, professional or not, takes part in, they have also resulted from bias in the U.S. system of psychodiagnosis, the most highly formalized system in the world. The process of diagnosis, whether informal or formal, is inevitably linked as much—if not more—to the personality, theoretical orientation, and cultural circumstances of the therapist (or whoever is the assessor) as it is to the personality and circumstances of the patient. This fact has often been overlooked throughout the history of the formation of diagnostic systems themselves.

Mental health professionals of all theoretical viewpoints have rarely acknowledged this fact. To this day, they frequently continue to ignore context, both personal and cultural. In contrast, this book will repeatedly emphasize context in its broadest sense, because historically so many women have endured negative consequences from its neglect. For the most part, the underlying diagnostic assumptions and the classifications derived from them have historically been developed by males—with little real awareness of female experience and, until recently, with practically no input from women.

One more important point about diagnosis will be emphasized throughout. No classification system that human beings have devised, whether to categorize plants and animals, to describe the descent of humans from our prehuman ancestors, or any other, perfectly describes the subject or accounts for all the data available.

Data about the individual case is always lost in some measure when classification occurs. Also, even in more definitive sciences such as botany, paleontology, and physical medicine, disputes arise about particular categories. Changes are made in the classification systems as new information becomes available. Note, too, that the classification system always describes the ideal case. Even in a field as definitive as anatomy, surgeons soon learn that the internal organs of one person are only approximately where they have seen them in textbooks. One person's heart or lungs or liver (even in a healthy person) are almost always a few degrees or centimeters away from where the ideal examples say they should be. Nevertheless, classification systems serve important professional purposes, a topic that will also be explored further later.

Compared with the physical sciences, our dilemmas in the mental health field are magnified because we have a much less definitive body of data on which to build classification schemas. Particularly here, almost no person is likely to fit the ideal case. Even more than in other fields, it is important for mental health professionals to remember that both the classification systems and any conclusion that any one person has symptoms that fit one or more categories within that system are opinions, not facts. Theories that lie behind classification systems always include opinion, often more opinion than verified fact. We hope, of course, that these opinions are at least educated guesses. Nevertheless, it has been common to find the labels within psychological diagnostic systems reified as if they represented material things in the real world. That some group of people originally got together to devise the labels is quickly forgotten, as is the methodology, whether opinion polling or anything else, used in the process. Some segments of the mental health professions themselves have reified their labels, and in general, to the disgrace of our field, diagnosis is frequently taught to budding mental health professionals as if it just existed de facto. New professionals often conclude that our diagnostic system came into existence in full bloom without any history and just is so. They often do not learn that context is a significant if unacknowledged variable. Like "hysteria" and the "wandering womb," diagnostic systems reflect the times and locations in which they are developed and used, and the values of those using them. Women scholars have documented that women's views have been discounted for thousands of years in the intellectual tradition that has called itself civilization (Boulding, 1992a, 1992b). It should be no surprise, then, to find that they have also been discounted in the particular case of mental illness classification systems.

Today, it is most often one person, sometimes a psychologist but usually a psychiatrist, who decides that one woman should have one particular label. The system that contains that label represents the collective opinion of a particular segment of the mental health field about which facts are relevant and how they should be ordered. The system, though, carries much patriarchal, stereotypic, and class baggage, and the claims its formulators make about its scientific validity and reliability are disputed (Kirk & Kutchins, 1992). Many segments of the mental health field have not participated in the establishment of the present system, nor does everyone agree with it or accept it in its totality.

One other significant problem that arises in the mental health field is that when a label or a category is assigned to a complex living, breathing, feeling human being, it has unintended consequences. Scientific classifications such as those mentioned earlier are unlikely to have any significant impact upon any particular living persons. Mental illness classifications, in contrast, are markedly different in that they do heavily impact the specific people being labeled. As I write this sentence, I am thinking particularly of a woman who was confined to a wheelchair by a variety of physical ailments. While she was naturally unhappy about her medical condition, she functioned well in the care home where she lived. A psychiatrist, new to the setting and the residents, was able to get this woman, who had no prior psychiatric history, committed to a mental hospital for depression—after just one encounter with her. She returned two weeks later to the home. She denied to me that she had been more depressed than usual or that she had been or was suicidal. After her return, she was more anxious and less self-confident than before being hospitalized. She unhappily told me that she didn't belong in a hospital with "crazy" people. I agreed with her. She had no power to determine or even influence the course of her hospital treatment, a fact that only demoralized her further by undermining any sense she had that she had some control over her own life.

At its best (but even this is far from always true), the initial act of labeling helps determine a course of treatment. But in addition to this, one result of labeling is that others react to the person not as a complex, often contradictory, being but as if she or he personified the label. Like the woman in the care home, persons designated as patients often find their humanity reduced to a hypothesized disease process. Unfortunately, this can happen throughout medicine, but it is more significant and perhaps more poignant when it happens in the mental illness area. Often, patients are not seen as anything more than a label by those mental health personnel who adhere most rigidly to the prescribed schema of the time. Many mental patients who have been thus labeled have told of their experiences. Their accounts give us a glimpse into the situation of myriads who have not been able to share their individual stories about similar experiences.

One additional terrible consequence is that the label, developed tentatively and perhaps even (sometimes) applied in a humane fashion, is taken as if it represented total, unchanging, absolute truth about human behavior, motives, and distress. Sometimes this happens outside the profession in how the public reacts to what it learns about "mental illness," but it also happens within these fields themselves.

Chapters 2 and 3 describe the history and development of our American diagnostic system. Because women have often been the primary patients throughout that history, the application of the system to women will be emphasized. Among the significant issues we will attend to in that history is that it was originally developed for one set of purposes and, in the present, is frequently used for a multiplicity of purposes that may have little direct relevance to the treatment of a specific human being. In addition, all of the peculiarities with which our cultural tradition has habitually viewed women have been incorporated, if not rigidly embedded, in the traditional forms, customs, and labels used in psychodiagnosis.

Recognizing that in general theory has followed practice, we will look in chapter 4 at the purposes of diagnosis as they have been described in the professional literature with a critical eye to what happens in the real world when diagnostic labels are affixed to human beings. We will explore the consequences of the wide gulf that has historically existed between how diagnoses were designed to be used and how they are actually used on a day-to-day basis. Most mental health practitioners are not even aware that the research literature includes some other thoughtfully developed possible alternatives to the present system. Chapter 5 will look at several of these in order to see what clinical use can be made of them. Chapter 6 will explore some of the larger issues involved in the process of diagnosis, for example, the trouble we still have with the very definition of "mental disorder."

We will end with a discussion of recent feminist perspectives on the diagnostic process in an attempt to incorporate the experience of both women patients and women professionals into the process—a process that in large measure has excluded us in the past and still does so in the present.

## CHAPTER 2

From Individual Opinion to Authoritarian Uniformity: The History of U.S. Classification Systems

SETTING THE CONTEXT

IT MAY SEEM ODD to view 1900 as prehistory, although for the purposes of mental disorder classification, it is just that. Almost all that is significant in the systematization of diagnosis has occurred during the twentieth century. Throughout the Western world, there was no standardization of mental diagnosis at the end of the nineteenth century. Every theorist, it seemed, had his (used advisedly) own system.

Physicians who specialized in mental illness were called alienists, although neurologists were also involved with mental matters. Brill (1972) tells us that the term *alienated* originated with the belief "that the victim had alienated or given over control of his soul to the devil in barter" (p. 187)—a definition that faintly echoes what, for want of a more specific term, can be called prescientific times when mental disorders were thought of primarily in religious terms. One need think only of European and early American purges of witches, many of whom were probably senile and/or self-sufficient older women (although others must have been women of any age who attempted to be independent and for that reason did not fit into the established cultural mode) and others who demonstrated classical hysterical symptoms (Veith, 1965).

11

In 1900, the United States was only a few decades from the Civil War and the emancipation of the slaves. Ostensibly we had moved into the era of scientific thought. Before the Civil War, Dr. Samuel Cartwright proposed two diagnoses for mental ailments that he suggested were prominent among the black slave population: drapetomania and dyaesthesia aethiopica. *Drapetomania* is still listed today in medical dictionaries and defined innocently in terms of its Greek roots as "the insane impulse to wander away from home" (Thomas, 1993). A current psychiatric dictionary defines it as the "uncontrollable impulse to wander," cross-referencing it to the terms *dromomania* and *simple senile deterioration* (Campbell, 1989). It is thus now designated as a symptom of organic dementia, and while the term is not often used today, Cartwright actually applied the term to runaway slaves! Dyaesthesia aethiopica, which is not found in current dictionaries, was also colloquially called "rascality" and apparently included all other behaviors that masters did not like in their slaves: talking back, fighting with owners, destroying plantation property, procrastinating, or refusing to work (Landrine, 1988). Other examples of the intrusion of general cultural racist views into the psychiatric view of black people have been well documented (Thomas & Sillen, 1972). We will see that this intrusion continues today.

Another example of the political use of diagnosis is "anarchia," named by Benjamin Rush, a signer of the Declaration of Independence and physician general of the Continental army, who is often considered the founder of American psychiatry. Anarchia, he said, was the form of insanity suffered by those who were dissatisfied with the new political structure of the United States and sought yet more democracy. Never mind that black slavery still existed, that only white males could vote, or that class divisions were prominent. Any wish for change represented a symptom of mental disease (Brown, 1990). *Anarchia*, derived of course from "anarchy," is not listed in current psychiatric dictionaries. At the time, though, this diagnosis reflected one person's political philosophy, a process not appreciably different from what can and still does occur today.

In a later instance, consider the view of Bruno Bettelheim (1969), a prominent psychiatrist and psychoanalyst, who in 1969 denied to the U.S. Congress that antiwar protesters at the University of Chicago had any serious political agenda. He indicated instead that in invading the dean's or president's office, violently, or by means of sit-ins [students, although] big in age and size . . . inwardly feel like little boys, and hence need to play big by sitting in papa's big chair. They want to have a say in how things are run, want to sit in the driver's seat, not because they feel competent to do so, but because they cannot bear to feel incompetent. (p. 407)

Nothing in what he said reflects the view of most people that the Vietnam war was unjust. His statements came from a typical application of psychoanalytic theory: The rebel wishes to supersede authority (his father). No information is ever included about whether the rebel is acting against forces that might truly be oppressive. This is a clear example of the neglect of the context surrounding actions.

None of these examples leads us to see the ways scientific thought has been applied to psychological issues in a positive light. Instead, each carries much baggage in the form of stereotypes that were part of the everyday culture and were unseen by proponents who believed themselves to be acting scientifically. With the advantage of time, we can relatively easily see the unexamined assumptions that led people to label undesired behavior as pathological and thereby control it. When we examine more current diagnostic circumstances, however, it is harder to sort out largely unexamined assumptions that remain and that limit and control the psychological freedom of underclasses (including women) today. Despite the media's focus on the diverse viewpoints of various interest groups, usually women and ethnic and racial minorities, only one accepted psychodiagnostic system, formulated primarily by affluent white males, remains as the measuring stick used to measure all groups.

One has only to look at the difficulty men have with the concept of sexual harassment (a concept outside the diagnostic schema). Differences in life experiences led women to complain that men just didn't "get it" when Anita Hill spoke up against Supreme Court Justice Clarence Thomas during his confirmation hearings. Women understood because many had lived through similar experiences. Similarly, blacks and whites differed in their reactions to the not guilty verdict for O. J. Simpson because blacks' differing experiences did not fit into the majority or mainstream (read "white") experience. Just as men generally do not acknowledge the trauma and disempowerment in women's lives because they cannot locate it in their own experience, whites generally cannot see the trauma and disempowerment in the lives of blacks and other minority groups. We live amid our own experience and our time's assumptions and cannot easily distance ourselves from them. It would be extremely foolish, as even these few instances illustrate, to assume that we have advanced to such a point that no blind spots remain in the supposedly scientific and objective endeavor of diagnostic classification.

Even if the examples given here were the only instances, it still would not be possible to accept the implicit message that all is well with mental illness classification and that it has never been used for social control. Yet even as we acknowledge our own lack of perfection, we must also recognize that our psychological and sociological awareness has increased immeasurably in the years since 1900. The status of women, although still far from perfect, has changed drastically during this century. Women today would not emotionally recognize the situation of women circa 1900 unless they were actively steeped in history. Women were all but chattels without the right to vote or to decide their futures or their children's futures without deference to husbands, fathers, or brothers. This status influenced how women were seen and labeled in terms of their mental health.

Women, for example, were diagnosed as mentally ill when they failed to perform their household duties, as defined by their husbands initially and then by usually male psychiatrists. Similarly, early psychiatrists often judged women's mental illness to be a result of undue mental exertion. As in the famous case of Charlotte Perkins Gilman, they frequently prescribed complete abstention from such activities as reading, studying, and writing to cure neurasthenia. Gilman spent one month in a sanitarium run by Dr. S. Weir Mitchell (about whom more later) and several months following his prescription at home before rebelling against it, leaving her first marriage and its circumscribed structure and largely recovering from her depressive and anxiety symptoms. In "The Yellow Wallpaper," Gilman (1899/1973) described a woman who became more and more demented when she was removed from her family and ordinary pursuits and allowed to do nothing except stare at the wallpaper. For Gilman, the story presented a view of what could have happened to her had she lacked the internal strength to reject the prescription of mental and physical inactivity. Later, in 1915, she published "Dr. Clair's Place," a story based on the treatment of neurasthenia by female doctors such as Mary Putnam Jacobi. Both the treatment and the outcome in this story were very different from those in "The Yellow Wallpaper." The treatment involved more empathy, human contact, and empowerment.

Also worthy of note is the case of Alice James, born in 1848, sister both to William James, a philosopher and psychologist, and to the writer Henry James. Despite being reared in the same household, one devoted to the life of the mind by their father, Henry James Sr., Alice spent most of her life as an invalid diagnosed at various times as having "neurasthenia, hysteria, rheumatic gout, suppressed gout, cardiac complication, spinal neurosis, nervous hyperesthesia, and spiritual crisis" (Strouse, 1980, pp. ix–x), a compilation that, among other things, illustrates the unsystematized state of diagnosis at the time. Her brothers attested to her brilliance and wit, but we have only her letters and the diary she kept during the last three years of her life (Yeazell, 1981). Despite neurasthenic-type symptoms that were also part of her brothers' lives, they did not become lifelong invalids, and her two other brothers engaged in a variety of external activities. Garth Wilkinson James was an adjutant with the first black Civil War regiment, married, and had children. Robertson James also served during the Civil War, married, and had children, but he was also hospitalized for a breakdown in 1888 (from which he seems to have recovered). According to Strouse (1980):

> "In our family group," wrote her novelist brother [Henry James], "girls seem scarcely to have had a chance." There was only one girl in the family circle. Her father viewed women as personifications of virtue, innocent purity, holy self-sacrifice. Boys had to learn to be good, through suffering and the interesting use of perception, but girls were good by nature and could dispense with interesting ideas. To be a James and a girl, then, was a contradiction in terms. And it is Alice's struggle to resolve that essential contradiction, her attempt to find something whole and authentic in her own experience, that gives her life its real stature and interest. (p. xiii)

Neurasthenia was first identified by George M. Beard in 1869 to designate a wide variety of symptoms for which no physical pathology could be found. Beard believed that it resulted when the demand for nervous energy exceeded the available supply. In Beard's long list of causes, "he gave special attention to the periodical press, steam power, the telegraph, the sciences, and the increased mental activity of women" (Sicherman, 1977, p. 35).

Beard treated men primarily, but S. Weir Mitchell, who invented the rest cure, had predominantly women patients. The diagnosis was at first limited to the upper classes until some of its proponents began to practice in public hospitals, giving them the opportunity to diagnose it among the lower classes as well.

Because neurasthenia's assumed physical basis was unproven, it began to disappear as a label after 1920 when its symptoms could be better explained by the psychodynamic views of Sigmund Freud. It briefly resurfaced, though, as a category in the 1968 version of the *Diagnostic and Statistical Manual* (American Psychiatric Association, 1968).

A BRIEF PREHISTORY

The attempt to categorize and classify mental disorders goes far back in history. The mental changes associated with old age were noticed early, although the technology that enables us to identify actual brain changes correlated with such behavior is fairly recent. Changes resulting from alcohol use were also noted early. Early cultures also recognized deliria resulting from fever, some depressive states, epilepsy, psychosomatic effects, malingering, and mental retardation (Brill, 1972).

In the fifth century B.C.E. Hippocrates developed one of the first categorizations of mental illness, based on clinical differences he observed. His very basic system included epilepsy, mania, melancholia, and paranoia. Aretaeus was next after Hippocrates, and in the first century A.D. studied patients over time. He saw that some people had periods of both mania and depression, separated by times of health. He also learned and passed on the perception that not all mental illness inevitably led to deterioration (Singerman, 1981).

Modern classification efforts in the sciences began in the late eighteenth century with Linnaeus, who tackled biological taxonomy. In 1769 William Cullen coined the word *neurosis* as part of his attempt to catalog mental diseases the way Linnaeus had cataloged biological entities. In Cullen's view, neurosis had a biological basis in the action of the nervous impulse. As he defined it, it contained most of what we would now call neurological, psychosomatic, neurotic, and psychotic disorders. He subdivided neurosis into four orders: comas (including apoplexy), adynamias (including hypochondriasis), spasms (including convulsions and hysteria), and vesanias ("an old term for full-fledged mental disorder, marked by the four stages of mania, melancholia, paranoias, and dementia" [*Dorland's Illustrated Medical Dictionary*, 1965, p. 1686]). Cullen also extended the ancient view of hysteria as a uterine disorder to include the ovaries; thus he was indirectly responsible for the thousands of oophorectomies (removal of ovaries) and clitoridectomies (removal of clitorises) performed in the nineteenth century on "hysterical" women (Knopf, 1970).

It was, however, the establishment of mental asylums where the mentally ill could be systematically observed that spurred the development of psychiatric nosology. Pinel, in France, was one of the first to develop a system based on his own observations. He noted the existence of melancholia, mania without delirium, mania with delirium, dementia, and idiotism. He mentioned mental indispositions and the mental changes of age, although he did not describe them. He worked in the early nineteenth century and was influenced by Thomas Sydenham's earlier stress on the importance of careful and what were considered to be nonbiased observations.

In the second half of the nineteenth century, Griesinger in Germany developed an influential classification system for organic disorders. Others, some of whose names live on in psychiatric diseases named for them, included Alzheimer, Nissl, Wernicke, Bonhoeffer, and Korsakoff. Meanwhile, Itard and Sequin clarified mental deficiency.

The term *dementia praecox* was first used by Morel in 1850, although he did not describe it. Hecker and Kahlbaum labeled katatonia (usually spelled *catatonia* in more recent times) in 1870. The modern pioneer, however, was Kraepelin, the person to whom most current attempts to classify mental disorders refer. He brought katatonia, hebephrenia, various dementias, vesanias, and certain degenerations together to fully create the clinical concept of dementia praecox (later modified to schizophrenia by Bleuler). He also gave us the basic delineation of the manic-depressive psychoses (recently relabeled bipolar disorders). A significant part of identification of an entity for Kraepelin involved its eventual outcome.

Despite the term's early use by Cullen, neurosis as we think of it today is a relatively late development as a psychiatric concept. Although neurosis is related to the ancient concept of hysteria and to the work of Mesmer's followers in the nineteenth century, it took root with the work of Beard in neurasthenia, Janet in psychasthenia, and Charcot in hysteria. It was Sigmund Freud, however, who fully described its symptoms and presumed etiology. Although it had a major indirect influence on psychiatric classification, Freud's psychoanalytic theory has existed and continues to exist in a totally separate realm parallel to formal, official psychiatric diagnosis. Freudian theory has survived in pop culture, however, in two particular ways: It has made it easy to label women's actions "hysterical"; and, before the onset of the current women's movement, it led to the belief that assertive women experience penis envy, a term that has never actually appeared in a diagnostic manual.

In the United States, the National Committee for Mental Hygiene began in 1917 to publish the *Statistical Manual for the Use of Hospitals in Mental Diseases*. This was a first step toward diagnostic standardization in psychiatry. Although its purpose was primarily to collect statistics, it provided a rudimentary nomenclature and classification system for hospitalized mental patients that was periodically revised and updated. Most of its original categories were based on the belief that mental disorders had a biological basis. They included such labels as traumatic psychoses, senile psychoses, manic-depressive psychoses, dementia praecox, paranoid conditions, epileptic psychoses, psychoneuroses, and neuroses, psychopathic inferiority, and psychoses with mental deficiency.

Lending insight into the thinking that went into the manual are reports and discussions among psychiatrists at the time that have been preserved in the transactions of the American Medico-Psychological Association. After original categories were reported to the association in 1917 (Salmon et al., 1917), the process of diagnosis was discussed by Southard in 1918 after an informal poll of fellow psychiatrists. He found what he considered "extraordinary unanimity" (p. 270) among American psychiatrists on the basics of nosology, although they diverged as to nomenclature. From this distance in time, it is difficult to determine exactly what he meant. Southard also proposed some small changes to render the system more practically useful (Southard, 1918). Orton, in opposition, tried to reorder the system along more theoretical lines, commenting to Southard that "the practical of to-day is the obsolete of to-morrow" (Orton, 1919, p. 417). Farrer, one of the discussants of Orton's paper, suggested the need to synthesize "our diagnoses from the returns of the pathologist and physiologist, the chemist and the psychologist" (Orton, 1919, p. 415), something that has never been accomplished to date but still sounds like a potentially good idea. This dispute could still take place today, for at bottom it suggests that not one of the professionals at that time showed that he had any idea that he was classifying human beings. Even Farrer only wished to include data from the other acknowledged sciences.

The manual went through 10 editions between 1918 and 1942, although its categories remained essentially the same until the 8th edition in 1934 (May et al., 1934), when it incorporated the Standard Nomenclature of Disease developed by the American Psychiatric Association (once called the American Medico-Psychological Association and earlier still, illustrating its origins, the Association of Medical Superintendents of American Institutions for the Insane [Barton, 1987]). The association maintained a Committee on Statistics whose work interfaced with the publication of the *Statistical Manual* by the National Committee for Mental Hygiene, leading to the change. By the time of its 10th edition, psychoneuroses and primary behavior disorders were more fully delineated (Grob, 1991).

American psychiatry, under the influence of Adolph Meyer, a prominent early American psychiatrist, was originally imbued with the belief that mental ills had biological causes. Until World War II, the influences of organic thought clearly determined the form of psychiatric diagnoses. World War II, though, exposed psychiatrists to other populations than the hospitalized at a time when psychoanalytic and other psychodynamic formulations of nonorganic problems were becoming more influential (American Psychiatric Association, 1952). This influence colored the original *Diagnostic and Statistical Manual* of the American Psychiatric Association issued in 1952 and played a major role in the drafting of *DSM-II*.

> Psychiatry itself was born out of classification. Europe was its birthplace, and European nosologists were its founding fathers. (Stefanis, 1988, p. xi)

DEVELOPMENT OF *DSM-I*

Just as it spurred many other changes in the mental health field, World War II served as an impetus to a greater focus on diagnosis, particularly of psychiatric disorders that did not require extensive hospital care. Oddly, though, from 1942 to 1952, four different classification systems that alternately expanded and contracted the psychoneurotic categories were formulated and in use. The first was the 1942 Standard Nomenclature of Diseases, a revision of the 1934 classification previously mentioned. In this edition, 24 categories were divided into five major sections. One of these was psychoneuroses, which included hysteria (anxiety hysteria, conversion hysteria, and subgroups), psychasthenia or compulsive states (and subgroups), hypochondriasis, reactive depression, anxiety state, anorexia nervosa, and mixed psychoneurosis.

A second system was the War Department Nomenclature (1945), which included the following under psychoneurotic reactions: anxiety reaction, dissociative reaction, phobic reaction, conversion reaction, somatization reactions (with subdivisions into psychogenic gastrointestinal reaction, psychogenic cardiovascular reaction, psychogenic genitourinary reaction, psychogenic allergic reaction, psychogenic asthenic reaction), obsessive–compulsive reaction, hypochondriacal reaction, and neurotic depressive reaction.

The nomenclature of the Veterans Administration published in 1947 is very similar to that of the War Department. It followed a similar pattern but subdivided conversion reaction into anesthetic type, paralytic type, hyperkinetic type, paresthetic type, autonomic type, and mixed type. It also subdivided the somatization reactions even more specifically than by reference to the particular body system involved. Asthenic reaction was separately classified.

Out of the War Department and Veterans Administration nomenclatures emerged a fourth system, the American Psychiatric Association's *Diagnostic and Statistical Manual,* published in 1952. Still largely oriented toward disorders requiring hospitalization, the original *DSM* also included sections on neurotic, psychophysiologic, transient situational, and personality disorders. These categories were included in direct response to the new requirements that had arisen during the wartime practice of psychiatry. Additionally, the *DSM* condensed the subheadings of the psychoneurotic disorders into anxiety reaction, dissociative reaction, conversion reaction, phobic reaction, obsessive–compulsive reaction, depressive reaction, and other psychoneurotic reactions.

Illustrating the turmoil brought about by these contrasting systems was the fact that the 1942 Standard Nomenclature was used in New York State until 1968 and the publication of *DSM-II* (Spitzer & Wilson, 1968). Amazingly, during these years *DSM-I* was officially accepted everywhere in the United States except in the state of New York. But despite these efforts to advance the state of psychiatric classification, from the viewpoint of women and members of minority cultural groups, there was no advance. The cultural views of majority (white male) society were incorporated into the original *DSM* as they had been into its forerunners. Whatever advances in diagnostic nomenclature occurred were a result of clinical work with the predominantly male population of the armed services as they responded to their experiences with combat and combat-related injuries.

Work with the concept of a psychiatric traumatic disorder, although not so named and not formally incorporated into the official psychiatric classification until 1980, had already begun. It had been spurred both by earlier wartime experiences and by the development of workers' compensation systems for work injuries. F. W. Mott had coined the term "shell shock" in 1919 and suggested that it resulted from a physical change in the brain brought about by carbon monoxide or changes in atmospheric pressure. Others later suggested that in most cases it had psychological causes related to experiences of horror and fright. Abraham Kardiner in 1941 suggested that war trauma was no different from other traumas such as those caused by industrial, road, and railway accidents. These were still being designated as falling under the rubric of neurosis as a category and generally labeled traumatic neuroses (Trimble, 1985), a designation Freud had originated to differentiate "real" neurosis from psychoneurosis.

The original *DSM* did contain a section labeled transient situation personality disorders. It included the diagnosis of gross stress reaction, which was

> justified only in situations in which the individual has been exposed to severe physical demands or extreme emotional stress, such as in combat or in civilian catastrophe (fire, earthquake, explosion, etc.). In many instances this diagnosis applies to previously more or less "normal" persons who have experienced intolerable stress. (American Psychiatric Association, 1952, p. 40)

I received my original training when *DSM-I* was in use. I do not recall any mention of this diagnosis nor of hearing of anyone who was given it, although I interned in Veterans Administration hospitals, probably the most likely place to find persons with such a label at that time. This diagnosis prefigures posttraumatic stress disorder, which originated in *DSM-III* but does not seem to have been widely used, probably because recognition of traumas had not sufficiently progressed. Certainly, no one was publicly commenting on the traumas in the daily lives of women and minority males, much less any sexual and violent trauma to which these groups and others could be subject. Even the wartime traumas of soldiers and allied personnel were not yet sufficiently meaningful to those doing the classifying.

The International Classification of Diseases and Causes of Death, later amended to the International Classification of Diseases, Injuries and Causes of Death (ICD), was first adopted in 1893. It was not until its sixth revision in 1946 that mental disorders were included. The ICD–6, published in 1948, closely paralleled the system used by the U.S. War Department (Kramer, 1988).

DEVELOPMENT OF *DSM-II*

By the time the original *Diagnostic and Statistical Manual* was superseded by *DSM-II* in 1968, greater attempts were made to have its nomenclature conform to the International Classification of Diseases (ICD), then in its eighth edition. In *DSM-II*, the categories of both personality disorders and psychoneurotic disorders (although the specific entities were called reactions in line with the theories of Adolph Meyer) were expanded. These "reactions" were labeled neuroses and classified as follows: anxiety neurosis, hysterical neurosis (subdivided into conversion type and dissociative type), phobic neurosis, obsessive–compulsive neurosis, depressive neurosis, neurasthenic neurosis, depersonalization neurosis, hypochondrical neurosis, and "other" neurosis. The presumed etiology of these disorders was often given, stated primarily in psychoanalytic terms.

Categories for "Certain Other Non-Psychotic Mental Disorders" were added (and distinguished, at least in concept, from personality disorders). These included sexual deviations, alcoholism, and drug dependence. "Special Symptoms," also delineated separately, included speech disorders, sleep and eating orders, enuresis, and so forth. Separate categories called "Behavior Disorders of Childhood and Adolescence" and "Conditions Without Manifest Psychiatric Disorder and Non-Specific Conditions" were also added. The latter section included social maladjustments without manifest psychiatric disorder, marital maladjustment, social maladjustment, occupational maladjustment, dyssocial behavior, and a category for other social maladjustment. For the first time, provision was made to indicate whether brain syndromes were acute or chronic, whether disorders were in remission, and also to rate them as mild, moderate, or severe.

Until *DSM-III* was published in 1980, no attempts were made to formulate the classification system upon other than the collective impressions of groups of psychiatrists. After *DSM-II* was formulated, drafts of it were circulated to 120 prominent psychiatrists for comment. And comment they did—with as many urging inclusion of more specific nosological entities as opposing the inclusion of particular categories. The greatest heat and tension, however, was caused by an internal private argument about whether American psychiatry would be served or hindered by having its system conform to the ICD, the International Classification of Diseases (Letters to Ernest Gruenberg, chair of the Committee on Nomenclature and Statistics from Walter Barton, 3/29/67; Bernard Bandler, 4/5/67; Leo Bartemeier, 3/30/67; John Blasko, 4/7/67; Norman Cameron, 4/10/67, 4/23/67; Eugene Brody, 3/15/67; Aaron Satloff and John Romano, 3/22/67; Mabel Ross, 4/21/67; Jurgen Ruesch, 3/15/67; George Stevenson, 4/6/67; John Whitehorn, 3/19/67; Lawrence Kolb, 6/26/67; on file in the Archives of the American Psychiatric Association, Washington, DC).

In 1974, the American Psychiatric Association's board of trustees voted to eliminate the category for homosexuality from the sexual deviations section and to substitute the category of sexual orientation disorder. The new designation was designed to include only those who were disturbed by their homosexual orientation. The change came about following intense political dispute within the association. This was the first time, but not the last, that social movements external to the formal diagnostic process influenced and changed the results and, to some extent at least, the process. Because it originated primarily outside of professional circles, this debate was different from what happened later when feminists objected to proposed diagnoses for *DSM-III-R*. It was similar, however, in that a significant minority within the organization accepted and championed the external movement's ideas.

The Gay Liberation movement officially started with the Stonewall riots of 1969 in New York. In accord with the general political agitation for social change in the late 1960s, the movement took fire and male homosexuals and lesbians began to fight publicly for their civil rights and the removal of the stigma of mental illness that the *DSM* label gave them. As it happened, the American Psychiatric Association's 1970 convention was held in San Francisco, a hotbed of gay activity. Gay activists disrupted sessions dealing with the treatment of homosexuals and presented their demands to be part of a panel at the following year's meeting. Following additional disruption at the 1971 meeting and a panel whose topic was "Lifestyles of Non-Patient Homosexuals," the demand for deletion of the homosexual label from *DSM* was made.

At the 1972 convention, one panel included a hooded Dr. Anonymous, who identified himself as a homosexual psychiatrist and told the group that more than 200 such psychiatrists were attending that convention. After this meeting the formal process for removing the homosexual label from *DSM* was begun. Ronald Bayer's detailed history of the process that ensued (Bayer, 1981) provides a good example of how social forces can influence diagnostic categorization.

DEVELOPMENT OF *DSM-III*

The American Psychiatric Association's philosophy of classification changed in several ways between *DSM-II* and *DSM-III*. The introduction to *DSM-III* explains that it attempted to be descriptive and atheoretical with respect to the etiology of disorders. The subdivisions of each diagnostic class, greatly expanded over *DSM-II*, represented what the working task force thought would be most useful. The writers of *DSM-III* provided explicit criteria for each disorder and contrasted this with the absence of criteria in *DSM-I*, *DSM-II*, and ICD–9. Klerman (1986) touted it for reaffirming the concept of multiple single and separate disorders, for incorporating operational criteria for both inclusion and exclusion, for using description rather than inferences, for using reliability trials, and for its multiaxial system.

DSM-III was consciously formulated to "reflect the most current state of knowledge regarding mental disorders while maintaining compatibility with ICD–9" (American Psychiatric Association, 1980, p. 2). Its format, however, was very different from that of ICD. A great effort was made to increase the scientific rigor of diagnostic categories and differentiation among diagnoses. It was felt, however, that the earlier accordance of *DSM-II* with ICD–8 had been forced and artificial and therefore detrimental to diagnostic processes in the United States. The introduction to *DSM-III* indicated that the ICD–9 "did not seem sufficiently detailed for clinical and research use" (p. 2) in the United States, so categories were expanded, and the developing *DSM-III* categories were included in the ICD–9CM (CM standing for clinical modification), prepared by the Council on Clinical Classifications for the U.S. National Center for Health Statistics.

Beginning in the 1950s, in Boston and then in St. Louis, a group of research psychiatrists developed a process of systematically studying patients by using structured interviews. They developed specific diagnostic criteria for hysteria, anxiety neurosis, schizophrenia, manic-depressive psychosis, antisocial personality, phobias, and other diagnostic entities. Their results, published in 1972, were called the Feighner criteria after the senior author (Feighner et al., 1972). Later Robert Spitzer and his co-workers revised the research, which became known as the Research Diagnostic Criteria, or RDC (Spitzer, Endicott, & Robins, 1978). The group formulated 25 major diagnostic categories, many of which were divided into subtypes. Their major purpose was to enable investigators to select relatively homogeneous groups of subjects who meet specified diagnostic criteria referring to either symptoms, signs, duration, or course of illness, or to levels of severity of impairment. For some of the diagnoses, certain symptoms or symptom patterns have diagnostic significance only if they persist beyond a stated duration.

> In selecting the specific criteria for a given diagnostic category, an attempt was made to operationally define the category in a manner that would achieve maximal acceptance among clinicians and researchers who use that particular concept. . . .
>
> Special attention was given to reliability. The criteria were continually revised until it appeared that further revisions would not increase reliability without a loss of validity. (Spitzer, Endicott, & Robins, 1978, p. 774)

Although the overlap was not complete, the RDC became the basis upon which *DSM-III* was built under Spitzer's direction. It is worth noting that the criteria for each diagnosis were developed for research and not directly for clinical purposes.

DSM-III was, in general, much more detailed and specific than *DSM-II*. In the nonorganic psychoses section, separate categories for schizophrenic disorders and major affective disorders were delineated, each having many more and specific subheadings. A category called anxiety disorders included many subheadings previously listed as psychoneuroses. A separate category of phobic disorders was delineated, as was one for dissociative disorders and one for posttraumatic stress disorders, all under the overall heading of anxiety disorders. The personality disorders section was expanded into a variety of subtypes, sexual deviations was renamed paraphilias (a unique instance of a return to a Latinism), and a new category of gender identity disorders was included. The drug dependence section was renamed Substance Use Disorders and the subcategories expanded. Psychophysiological disorders could now be listed as psychological factors affecting physical condition, and the section entitled Special Symptoms was greatly expanded. Transient situational disturbances were relabeled Adjustment Reactions (the term originally used in the *DSM-I*) and subtyped by predominant symptomatology. A category entitled Impulse Disorders was added, including pathological gambling, kleptomania, pyromania, and isolated explosive disorder. Codings for "Conditions Not Attributable to a Mental Disorder" were expanded and the heading changed from Social Maladjustments without Manifest Psychiatric Disorder.

For the first time, *DSM-III* also relied upon a system of trials among mental health workers in an attempt to validate agreement on labels in the field—that is, in the hospitals where psychiatrists and others actually have to come up with particular diagnoses for particular patients. The correspondence related to *DSM-III*'s formulation also makes it clear that for the first time the political implications of the diagnostic process and of particular labels were being recognized, although minimally. The formulators of the system at least recognized that attaching a diagnosis to a person had implications beyond the manual.

By now, of course, the *Diagnostic and Statistical Manual* had become a standard recognized far beyond the American Psychiatric Association. It influenced insurance reimbursement of inpatient and outpatient treatment and our entire legal system. Although it was published in 1980, when the feminist movement was well under way, *DSM-III* did practically nothing (with the possible exception of the muting of some overt sexism in some descriptions) to demonstrate awareness of what the mental health field was already beginning to learn about women.

The fight between the psychoanalytically oriented psychiatrists and others that had surfaced over homosexuality in *DSM-II* continued throughout the process of drafting *DSM-III*. Although psychoanalysts were asked many times to come up with a standard nomenclature in accord with psychoanalytic theory, they never did. The more "pragmatically" oriented psychiatrists won the battle here, making *DSM-III* more behaviorally based than its predecessors, deliberately omitting psychodynamically based etiologic formulations for its diagnostic entities, practically eliminating the use of the term *neurosis,* and expanding the outpatient categories. Originally, the plan was to eliminate the term entirely, but because of the uproar from the psychoanalytic camp, a compromise was reached that differentiated between *neurotic disorder* and *neurotic process. Neurotic disorder* is the term used to describe what were previously known as the symptoms of neurosis. *Neurotic process* refers to the standard psychoanalytic understanding about etiology. It is not referred to in *DSM-III*, but it remained available for use by clinicians inclined toward this theory (Townsend & Martin, 1983).

In *DSM-III*'s multiaxial system of classification, the influence of social stressors was formally incorporated for the first time in ratings to be made on a separate axis (IV). One of the most important innovations was the differentiation between psychiatric diagnoses that were to be coded on axis I and those to be coded on axis II. Axis I is for symptomatic diagnoses such as depression and schizophrenia, whereas axis II (in adults) is reserved for the personality disorders that are seen as long-term modes of adaptation and are not considered to be symptomatic per se. Axis III is for any nonpsychiatric medical disorders considered to be clinically relevant to axis I and axis II diagnoses. Axis IV, as noted, measures the degree of influence of social stressors, and axis V is a rating of the general level of functioning.

An early proponent of multiaxial classification, by way of a word of caution, pointed out that the meaning of *axis* as it was used in *DSM-III* was unclear and that, in reality, it here meant only an aspect related to the individual rather than a dimension, as in most classification systems. He pointed out also that the predictive value of the additional axes was unknown, that there were no procedures for weighting the information of different axes in order to arrive at an integrated solution, and that rather than being a truly multiaxial system, the first axis of *DSM-III* contained more or less traditional psychiatric diagnoses (Helmchen, 1983). He turned out to be correct as far as the usage of *DSM-III* is concerned. Axes I and II are widely used, while only rarely are axes III, IV, and V formally considered. Issues pertaining to axis II will be discussed later.

Following the introduction of *DSM-III*, mental health professionals had to be retrained because of its major differences from *DSM-II* and the initial perceptions of professionals that it was more difficult to use. Further, the content of professional debate changed as the categories changed. Earlier arguments had been about such issues as the subcategories of schizophrenia. Now debates raged about the relatively new category of borderline personality disorder and how it fit into the schema. Although *DSM-III* did not use the word *neurosis*, the categories customarily subsumed under it were expanded further, paralleling the greater movement of psychiatrists into the private practice (outpatient) sector. The idea that there were nonpathological psychological problems (incorporated minimally in the previous *DSMs*) was expanded greatly with the implication that addiction to smoking, social and family conflicts, and the like were amenable to psychiatric treatment.

Robert Spitzer has been active on the American Psychiatric Association's Committee on Nomenclature and Statistics since *DSM-II* was drafted. He was the guiding force behind the *DSM-III* and *DSM-III-R* and their changes from earlier diagnostic manuals published by the association. Although social factors have been incorporated somewhat, Dr. Spitzer and his group do not seem to have been very attuned to the influence of social forces in the diagnostic process itself or in the formulation of diagnostic categories, nor to have considered that diagnosis can be subtly used for social control. An illustration of this appears in his rebuttal and counterrebuttal of David Rosenhan's work, which will be discussed in more detail in chapter 3 (Rosenhan, 1973, 1975; Spitzer, 1975, 1976).

The introduction to *DSM-III* states that it "is atheoretical with regard to etiology or pathophysiological process except for those disorders for which this is well established and therefore included in the definition of the disorder" (American Psychiatric Association, 1980, p. 7). Salzinger (1986) pointed out that this statement should not blind us to what the theoretical bases of the manual actually were. He suggested that:

> They are the basic medical assumptions about abnormal behavior: that it represents a sign or a symptom, that it is part of a "mental" disorder, that the signs are objective (presumably observed by the examiner) indicators, and that the symptoms are the subjective complaints by the patient. This is not simply a classification empirically arrived at. It is based on a theory that signs and symptoms are not important in and of themselves, but that we must look for some underlying cause, which in the current scene means a biochemical one or (still) a concept such as "anxiety." (Salzinger, 1986, pp. 115–116)

DEVELOPMENT OF *DSM-III-R*

Changes in *DSM-III* were made, and *DSM-III-R* (for revised) was published in 1987. As its designation indicates, it was not considered a major new edition. A group of sleep disorders in the appendix of *DSM-III* was incorporated into the body of *DSM-III-R*, the rating scale for axis V (a rating of highest adaptive functioning within a year previous to diagnosis) was expanded, several new diagnoses for organic disorders induced by specific psychoactive substances was introduced, and the details of the name or description of several disorders were changed. It was supposed to be nothing more than a refinement and minor retooling of *DSM-III*.

The process of this revision, however, generated a very public fight about the potential incorporation of three new diagnoses that feminist mental health workers felt would be particularly detrimental to women. The original proposal was to include masochistic personality disorder, paraphilic rapism, and premenstrual dysphoric disorder. In the end, these were listed in the appendix for further study. Premenstrual dysphoric disorder was relabeled late luteal phase dysphoric disorder, self-defeating personality disorder was substituted for masochistic personality disorder, paraphilic rapism was renamed sexual coercive disorder, and a category called abusive personality disorder (i.e., sadistic personality) was added. For the second time (the first was with gay rights activists in the early 1970s), the disputes were not primarily among psychiatrists and therefore unknown to the public at large. This time, women mental health professionals, both psychiatrists and psychologists, actively and openly protested the newly proposed diagnoses, which they viewed as being unfair to women. The Committee against Ms. Diagnosis picketed the American Psychiatric Association convention in Washington, DC, in May 1986. (This author was among the picketers.) Many major news weeklies and some daily newspapers reported this protest.

Masochism is a red-flag word for feminist therapists. Although Krafft-Ebing originated the word at the end of the last century (Widiger, 1987), we identify it largely with Freud. Freud identified primary pleasure in pain in three principal circumstances unique to women: castration (since, in his view, all women had been castrated), copulation, and childbirth. Helene Deutsch elaborated on the role of masochism in the normal life of women (Lerman, 1986), and the word had come to be almost exclusively used in diagnosing women. The proposed masochistic personality disorder did use the word in a less sexualized and somewhat more operational fashion than Freud did to refer to what mainstream male psychiatrists saw as self-defeating behaviors in women. Problems, however, remained with it. The general diagnostic criteria listed in the appendix of *DSM-III* for self-defeating personality disorder were:

> A pervasive pattern of self-defeating behavior, beginning by early adulthood and present in a variety of contexts. The person may often avoid or undermine pleasurable experiences, be drawn to situations or relationships in which he or she will suffer, and prevent others from helping him or her. (American Psychiatric Association, 1987, p. 373)

As a result of the intervention of feminists, it was added that this diagnosis was not to be used when the behaviors

> occur exclusively in response to, or in anticipation of, being physically, sexually, or psychologically abused. (American Psychiatric Association, 1987, p. 374. See also Kass, Spitzer, Williams, & Widiger, 1989, for comments on the response to the opponents of the diagnosis)

Feminists pointed out that women might not reveal the relevant abuse information to male psychiatrists, both because they do not routinely ask the appropriate questions and also because they are often reluctant to admit such abuse, points that made this diagnostic label even more problematic (Caplan, 1987; Rosewater, 1987). They also commented that this diagnosis stigmatized women for self-effacing behavior and other traits that women are socialized to have in our society (Carmen, 1985). Lenore Walker (1985) also disputed that the behavior in question was characterological, indicating that instead it changed when women's situations changed.

The issues for premenstrual dysphoric disorder were somewhat different. Since Frank (1931) first described what he called premenstrual tension in 1931, there has been much interest in this potential syndrome. It is fairly well accepted at this point as a physical disorder (Keye, 1988). In this case, the protesters pointed out that little if any scientific validation has ever been found for the relationship between women's moods and their menstrual cycles, despite widespread popular belief in this relationship. They feared that this diagnosis might be misused to discriminate against women in job situations (Hamilton & Gallant, 1988). They also pointed out that no evidence suggests that cyclic changes cause depression, that the cycle-related symptoms women report are quite varied and variable even for a particular woman and do not always include depression, and that the reification of menstruation in a label ignores the role situational and social factors play in moods (Alagna & Hamilton, 1986; Hamilton & Gallant, 1988).

A major earlier review of the literature (Rubinow & Roy-Byrne,

1984, p. 168) had suggested that at least six relevant questions about the relationship of PMS to psychiatric disorders could not yet be satisfactorily answered:

1. Whether PMS and psychiatric disorders were concurrent but distinct disorders.
2. Whether PMS can mimic major psychiatric disorder.
3. Whether there is a premenstrual alignment of psychiatric disorders.
4. Whether there is premenstrual exacerbation of existing psychiatric disorders.
5. Whether PMS could be a sensitizing experience influencing the course of a major psychiatric syndrome.
6. Whether there is etiologic communality between PMS mood syndromes and major psychiatric syndromes.

With such major questions as yet unanswered, it was indeed difficult to meaningfully formalize such a disorder as the late luteal phase dysphoric disorder.

Jean Hamilton, a psychiatrist and prime mover in the debate over the *DSM-III-R* diagnoses, cited the portrayal of the PMS debate in the media as an example of how women's contributions to science are trivialized:

> Instead of using a neutral term such as the "opposition," scientists who opposed the diagnosis were labeled "antagonist(s)," and, instead of acknowledging a variety of scientifically based arguments, the antagonists were said simply to "complain" causing otherwise "reasonable people . . . to [turn their] back on hard scientific evidence." The overall thrust of these characterizations in the mainstream media is to create the impression that "feminists" have not made scientific arguments at all. (Hamilton, 1987/1988)

Other groups argued against the diagnosis of paraphilic rapism (sexual coercive disorder), which they saw as having the potential to provide a legal psychiatric defense against charges of rape. Sadistic personality disorder (abusive personality disorder) seems to have been added as a counterpart to masochistic personality disorder but was not discussed much (Keyser, 1986).

Feminist psychiatrists and psychologists presented position papers to the *DSM-III-R* committee particularly about the proposal to include masochistic personality disorder and premenstrual dysphoric disorder. They pointed out that battered women often exhibit symptoms that resemble those ascribed to self-defeating personality disorder, which represents a long, characteristic pattern since it was proposed as an axis II disorder, but that they show much change within a fairly short time after they are no longer in an abusive situation. They also indicated that women may stay in an abusive relationship for many reasons, behavior that may look self-defeating but that may actually be practical (financial need) and life preserving (where they fear that they or their children might be further harmed if they leave) (Rosewater, 1985). They also protested the poor research justification for premenstrual disorder and its discriminatory potential.

Seven feminist psychologists and psychiatrists were invited to a work group meeting to discuss the issues surrounding the issue of masochistic personality disorder. Lenore Walker wrote a humorous account of her visit to the committee meeting for the Feminist Therapy Institute newsletter (Walker, 1986). She described the process of refining the criteria for self-defeating personality disorder. Around the computers:

> Each shouted out ideas for criteria coming from their own experience. Entries were done quickly, by consensus, although Spitzer was definitely in control. No time for research data, no time to think about social consequences. If the behavior was observable in patients, then a nosology category could be created. If one of the committee members saw the behavior in themselves, however, out with that criterion! (Seriously; one criterion was dropped because a work group member piped up with "I do that sometimes." The institutionalization of the Us–Them phenomenon was amazing to behold.)
>
> We were permitted to join in, and from time to time one of us would get over her shock and do so. Some of it was funny, like when we asked if early morning jogging, football, mountain climbing, wearing high heels or girdles were self-defeating behaviors. No, to sports activities, we were told, and no, to high heels, since that was a goal directed activity (we never asked to what goal), but yes to wearing a girdle unless she was over the age of 70! Obviously, they hadn't read *Women's Wear Daily* predicting the return of the girdle. Finally, the issue of moral, ethical and legal responsibility for the consequences of the proposed diagnosis was raised by Lynne [Lynne Bravo Rosewater]. When the idea of our challenge with a lawsuit was raised, the fingers finally stopped over the keyboard and the meeting was declared over. (p. 1)

To be fair, we must add that Robert Spitzer wrote a letter to *Time* magazine denying that the sort of horse-trading described ever took place (Spitzer, 1985).

DEVELOPMENT OF *DSM-IV*

The machinery behind the publication of *DSM-IV* began to gear up at the time *DSM-III-R* was published. Task forces to study each diagnostic area and issue were formed. Periodic updates on the process were sent to everyone who expressed an interest in getting on the mailing list. The American Psychiatric Association in 1991 published an options book, detailing some of the possibilities for changes being considered, and in 1993 circulated a book detailing drafts for diagnostic criteria. Although several prominent members of the association saw no immediate need for it and believed that it could not be justified by the accumulated research data (Zimmerman, 1988), *DSM-IV* was formally introduced at the association's annual convention in May 1994 with the aim of having it become the formal nomenclature by January 1995.

DSM-IV used the same format as *DSM-III* (and *DSM-III-R*). Axis IV was expanded to identify areas of social stressors, and the rating system for axis V changed. In addition, a small number of specific diagnoses were changed as a result of new research data. Despite the fanfare and the length of time since the publication of *DSM-III*, the number and nature of the changes in *DSM-IV* were decidedly minor. Several changes, however, should be noted.

First, homosexuality is not even listed in the index of *DSM-IV*. As in *DSM-III*, it is possible to diagnose homosexuality as a "sexual disorder not otherwise specified" when the individual is in sufficient distress about his or her sexual orientation. Homosexuality was, however, listed in the index of the *DSM-III*.

For the first time, premenstrual syndrome has actually been listed among the regular categories. Although the decision was made not to include a full-blown separate category, it is listed as a subcategory of "Depressive Disorder Not Otherwise Specified." One cannot be directed to this category from the index, however, because the index directs the reader only to premenstrual dysphoric disorder in the appendix, which lists categories that were rejected for inclusion. No mention is made of suggestions in the literature that there may be (at least) two distinct subtypes of symptom patterns, one characterized by irritability and tension and the other by depression (Hamilton & Gallant, 1988).

A third significant change is one of criteria rather than the inclusion or exclusion of a particular category. According to *DSM-III*, posttraumatic stress disorder could be diagnosed when "The person has experienced an event that is outside the range of usual human experience and that would be markedly distressing to almost anyone" (*DSM-III*, p. 250). The statement is admittedly vague and subject to individual interpretation; in fact, research suggests that many normally expected events (e.g., grief) can result in PTSD-like symptoms on occasion. This author is one who has criticized this criterion (Lerman, 1989). A person is now considered to have been exposed to a traumatic event when "the person experienced, witnessed, or was confronted with an event or events that involved actual or threatened death or serious injury, or a threat to the physical integrity of self or others" (American Psychiatric Association, 1994, p. 427). The implications of this change will be discussed later.

Additional changes were of a more general nature. Perhaps most notable is the separation of bipolar disorder into bipolar I and bipolar II depending on whether manic or depressive symptomatology is predominant.

Notable also is the apparent abandonment of the concept of a hierarchy of disorders, which was an explicit part of the *DSM-III*s. This concept, described in the *DSM-III*, is that symptoms of disorders lower in the hierarchy can occur in disorders higher in the system and these other disorders should not be diagnosed if a higher-order diagnosis is made. Many exclusion criteria were included in *DSM-III* diagnoses, although many were dropped in *DSM-III-R*. This concept is missing, although without explanation, from *DSM-IV*.

This shift has led to an increasing amount of research in what is called comorbidity, the occurrence of two or more disorders in the same person. Many feel that this phenomenon has important implications for diagnosis and treatment. Most disorders show systematic correlations with specific other diagnoses or classes of diagnoses. Questions thus arise as to whether individuals have more than one disorder or whether the stated subdivisions are incorrect. Research has identified high current and/or lifetime rates of overlap for practically all axis I disorders and even higher rates for the axis II personality disorders. This phenomenon is associated with greater severity and therefore poorer prognosis (Clark,

Watson, & Reynolds, 1995). Seemingly, however, no one involved in this area of research has questioned the validity of the categories.

Before going on, it is necessary to counter the public professional view that the *DSM-IV* process was scientific and open to input. Paula Caplan, a psychologist who served as a consultant and adviser to two *DSM-IV* Revisions Task Force work groups—those for self-defeating personality disorder and late luteal dysphoric disorder—has publicly described her frustration at not receiving copies of relevant data being amassed by the groups and at not even being able to learn submission deadlines. She concluded that

> the Work Group's claim to base decisions in good scientific practices is unjustified. Many of their biases are obvious, some more blatant than others. Occasionally, they drop all pretense of fairness. (Caplan, 1991, p. 169)

In addition, Kirk and Kutchins (1995) noted

> Twenty years after the reliability problem became the central focus of DSM-III, there is still not a single multi-site study showing that DSM (any version) is routinely used with high reliability by regular mental health clinicians. Nor is there any credible evidence that any version of the manual has greatly increased its reliability beyond the previous version. The DSM revolution in reliability has been a revolution in rhetoric, not in reality. (p. 7)

## CHAPTER 3

The Procrustean Bed: The U.S. Diagnostic System Analyzed

CHANGES IN CATEGORIES OVER TIME

SEVERAL DIFFERENT GENERAL tendencies characterize the period of history we are examining. One was to change the name of a diagnostic entity, often because the original or early name had accumulated emotional connotations, usually negative, that a name change (it was hoped) would lessen or eliminate. In some instances, a professional term had been adopted by the popular culture and the psychiatric profession was perhaps embarrassed to continue to use it formally. Examples include such terms as idiot, imbecile, and moron, progressively changed over time to mental defective, mentally retarded, and developmentally disabled, the present designation. Hysteria is another example.

Another type of change that has occurred over time has been the more specific (and sometimes more behavioral) delineation of symptoms and the incorporation of new entities into the classification lexicon.

Major Current Categories

Depression

Although it has never appeared in any version of *DSM* as an official diagnosis, melancholia has a long history as a psychiatric concept and was originally synonymous with depression. It represents the extreme of what we would commonly recognize as depression today, referring primarily to the profoundly unhappy state of those who take no pleasure and receive no uplift of spirit and mood from aspects of life that ordinarily afford pleasure and satisfaction. It generally includes depressive delusions, decreased ability to function, and other serious difficulties. In the nineteenth century, melancholia was differentiated from melancholy, which was seen as a less extreme depressive state that still permitted the individual to tend to ordinary tasks of life and work, although with depressive affect pervading (Campbell, 1989).

The distinction between melancholia and melancholy is roughly comparable to the distinctions made in the earliest editions of the *DSM*s between psychotic and neurotic depressions. Psychotic depression is seen as more serious, involving thought disturbances as well as mood disturbances, and less likely to be precipitated by specific life events.

In *DSM-I*, psychotic depressive disorders included involutional psychotic reaction, manic-depressive reactions, and psychotic depressive reaction. The psychoneurotic section listed depressive reaction.

Involutional psychotic reaction was described as being most commonly characterized by depression and occurring in the involution, that period of life characterized by "retrogressive change in vital processes after their functions have been fulfilled, such as the change that follows the menopause" (Thomas, 1993, p. 1016). Although the description in *DSM-I* was not gender specific, this disorder was commonly attributed to women who had reached menopause and implicitly assumed to be the result of the cessation of production of female hormones such as estrogen. That this unwritten assumption underlay its description can be seen most clearly by the erroneous comment in *DSM-II* describing involutional melancholia (the name used in *DSM-II*) that this disorder had been included in *DSM-I* under disorders due to disturbances of metabolism, growth, nutrition, or endocrine function (American Psychiatric Association, 1968, p. 36). This was not its actual placement.

Except for names, *DSM-II* made few changes in the depression categories. As indicated, involutional psychosis became involutional melancholia. Also, depressive reaction became depressive neurosis, and cyclothymic personality (alternatively listed as affective personality) was added to the list of personality disorders. Cyclothymic personality was a category designed to describe those who experienced recurring and alternating periods of depression and elation that were not intense enough for the diagnosis of manic-depressive psychosis.

Between 1968, the publication date of *DSM-II*, and 1980 and the publication of *DSM-III*, many changes occurred in our society. These included the progress of the women's movement both outside and within the mental health professions and other civil rights movements. Specific research in the psychology of women had found that from an epidemiological perspective, depression was found more often in women than in men and was possibly even increasing (Weissman & Klerman, 1977, 1979). No foundation was discovered, however, for a separate diagnosis for depression during the involutional period of life (Gitlin & Pasnau, 1989).

In *DSM-III*, involutional melancholia was dropped as a diagnosis. Manic-depressive psychosis became bipolar disorder, and cyclothymic personality became cyclothymic disorder. Major depression could now be diagnosed with specifications as to remission, psychotic features, or melancholia (here used to mean loss of pleasure in most of one's activities). The new name for what had been depressive neurosis was dysthymic disorder. The diagnosis for adjustment reactions, a category for milder reactions used in *DSM-II*, could now be specified in terms of features, including depressed mood as opposed to anxious mood, or with mixed features.

In *DSM-III-R*, dysthymia was further subdivided into primary and secondary types and was to be specified as early (before age 21) or late onset (after age 21). In the primary type,

> the mood disturbance is not related to a preexisting, chronic, non mood, Axis I or Axis II disorder, e.g., Anorexia Nervosa, Somatization Disorder, a Psychoactive Substance Dependence Disorder, an Anxiety Disorder or rheumatoid arthritis (American Psychiatric Association, 1987, p. 233)

The secondary type could be related to a chronic, preexisting nonmood axis I or axis II diagnosis. An additional category, entitled Depressive Disorder Not Otherwise Specified, was added to cover disorders with depressive features that did not meet the stated criteria for any other specific disorder.

In *DSM-IV*, the major changes are the separation of bipolar disorder into bipolar I and bipolar II disorders, the introduction of bipolar disorder not otherwise specified, and substance-induced mood disorder. It also specifies various types of "depressive disorder not otherwise specified," a diagnosis introduced in *DSM-III*. Bipolar I disorder is designed for those who predominantly have manic episodes with occasional depressive episodes, while bipolar II disorder is for those who predominantly have depressive episodes with occasional manic or hypomanic episodes.

I have not commented much about the bipolar disorders because, even when they are diagnosed in women, the primary symptomatology is depressive. It is more common for males to have manic episodes than it is for women (Fogarty, Russell, Newman, & Bland, 1994). Perhaps the new differentiation into bipolar I and bipolar II will result in increased research on this difference. It is generally accepted that depression of whatever form occurs more often in women than in men (Weissman & Klerman, 1977, 1979; Rothblum, 1983). Different theories have variously related this to female physiology, to the social roles of women, and most recently to the high proportion of females who have experienced some type of abuse (Cutler & Nolen-Hoeksema, 1991; Hamilton & Jensvold, 1992). Kate Millett (1990) has given us a poignant description from the patient's viewpoint of her experiences with the system while she was diagnosed manic-depressive and later as having a bipolar disorder.

Under the heading Depressive Disorder Not Otherwise Specified, six examples are given. The most significant for our purposes is premenstrual dysphoric disorder. Here, the separate disorder of premenstrual or late luteal dysphoric disorder originally proposed for *DSM-III-R*—and opposed—is introduced as a depressive disorder. It is to be diagnosed when

> in most menstrual cycles during the past year, symptoms (e.g., markedly depressed mood, marked anxiety, marked affective lability, decreased interest in activities) regularly occurred during the last week of the luteal phase (and remitted within a few days of the onset of menses). These symptoms must be severe enough to markedly interfere with work, school, or usual activities and be entirely absent for at least 1 week postmenses. (American Psychiatric Association, 1994, p. 350)

In a list of criteria sets for further study in Appendix B of *DSM-IV*, premenstrual dysphoric disorder is listed separately, along with recurrent brief depressive disorder, minor depressive disorder, mixed anxiety–depressive disorder, and depressive personality disorder. (Others listed in this appendix that are pertinent to women's issues but do not necessarily fall in the depression category are factitious disorder by proxy, binge-eating disorder, and passive–aggressive personality disorder.)

Schizophrenia

When I began my training in psychology, I worked as an intern in Veterans Administration hospitals, as many if not most clinical psychology students did at that time. Most inpatients in mental hospitals at that time were diagnosed as schizophrenics. It was rare to run across a person who had been diagnosed as having a manic-depressive reaction of any type. The broad category for the diagnosis was rarely an issue. In *DSM-I*, schizophrenia was labeled schizophrenic reaction and subdivided into various types: simple, hebephrenic, catatonic, paranoid, acute undifferentiated, chronic undifferentiated, and schizoaffective. The terms hebephrenic, catatonic, and paranoid come from the earlier history of psychiatry and in particular followed Kraepelin's typology. The description in *DSM-I* of the general category follows:

> This term is synonymous with the formerly used term dementia praecox. It represents a group of psychotic reactions characterized by fundamental disturbances in reality relationships and concept formations, with affective, behavioral, and intellectual disturbances in varying degrees and mixtures. The disorders are marked by strong tendency to retreat from reality, by emotional disharmony, unpredictable disturbances in stream of thought, regressive behavior, and in some, by a tendency to "deterioration." The predominant symptomatology will be the determining factor in classifying such patients into types. (American Psychiatric Association, 1952, p. 26)

In addition to the general definition, it is worthwhile for our purposes to look into the descriptions for the acute undifferentiated type and the chronic undifferentiated type because of what happened as diagnostic thinking progressed in later years. Under acute, we find:

> These symptoms appear acutely, often without apparent precipitating stress, but exhibiting historical evidence of prodromal symptoms. Very often the reaction is accompanied by a pronounced affective coloring of either excitement or depression. The symptoms often clear in a matter of weeks, although there is a tendency for them to recur. Cases usually are grouped here in the

first, or an early, attack. If the reaction subsequently progresses, it ordinarily crystallizes into one of the other definable reaction types. (American Psychiatric Association, 1952, p. 27)

The chronic type referred to long-standing cases but also:

Patients presenting definite schizophrenic thought, affect and behavior beyond that of the schizoid personality, but not classifiable as any other type of schizophrenic reaction, will also be placed in this group. This includes the so-called "latent," "incipient," and "pre-psychotic" schizophrenic reactions. (American Psychiatric Association, 1952, p. 27)

Psychiatric medications, which have revolutionized the treatment especially of the hospitalized mentally ill, began to appear in the early 1960s. Their appearance did not seem to have affected the way schizophrenia was regarded when *DSM-II* was published in 1968. More attention was paid to the differences between thought and mood disorders in the definition:

The schizophrenias, in which the mental status is attributable primarily to a *thought* disorder, are to be distinguished from the *Major affective illnesses* which are dominated by a *mood* disorder [emphasis in original]. (American Psychiatric Association, 1968, p. 33)

The term now used was schizophrenia, no longer schizophrenic reaction. A category in addition to paranoid schizophrenia, called paranoid states, was established. The subcategories under schizophrenia were somewhat but not markedly changed. Acute schizophrenic episode was substituted for acute undifferentiated type. A new category, called schizophrenia, childhood type, was also added for cases in which symptoms appeared before puberty. Latent type and residual type were added, and schizoaffective type was subdivided into excited and depressed. Because of later changes, it is worth quoting from the description of the latent type:

This category is for patients having clear symptoms of schizophrenia but no history of a psychotic schizophrenic episode. Disorders sometimes designated as incipient, pre-psychotic, pseudoneurotic, pseudo-psychopathic, or borderline schizophrenia are categorized here. (This category includes some patients who were diagnosed in *DSM-I* under "Schizophrenic reaction, chronic undifferentiated type." Others formerly included in that *DSM-I* category are now classified under *Schizophrenia, other [and unspecified] types* [sic].) (American Psychiatric Association, 1968, p. 34)

In *DSM-III*, the schizophrenias became schizophrenic disorders. The Kraepelinian subtypes became less important. The subtypes now listed were disorganized, catatonic, paranoid, undifferentiated, and residual, with chronicity and remission diagnosed in the numbering system rather than by the diagnosis itself. The most important change, however, was in how the label was to be used. It could not be used for illnesses of less than six months' duration. These were now to be identified as schizophreniform disorders, a term originated by Gabriel Langfeldt, a Norwegian psychiatrist (Rieder, 1974). Also:

> The approach taken here excludes illnesses without overt psychotic features, which have been referred to as Latent, Borderline, or Simple Schizophrenia. Such cases are likely to be diagnosed in this manual as having a Personality Disorder such as Schizotypal Personality Disorder. (American Psychiatric Association, 1980, p. 181)

Langfeldt had differentiated between a true schizophrenia, which always progressed toward deterioration, and the schizophreniform state, which looked like schizophrenia but had a more positive prognosis. When his ideas were incorporated into the *DSM*, they influenced how personality disorders were diagnosed as well. This aspect of the changes will be discussed later.

In *DSM-III-R*, the category again reverted to the term schizophrenia. Its subtypes remained the same, as did schizophreniform disorder. A separate delusional (paranoid) disorder was added with the possibility of specifying the type as erotomanic, grandiose, jealous, persecutory, somatic, and unspecified. Schizoaffective disorder, which could now be specified as bipolar type or depressive type, was still classified as one of the affective psychoses.

In *DSM-IV*, schizophrenia and "other psychotic disorders" (with the exception of the mood disorders, but not schizoaffective disorder) are grouped together. There are now brief psychotic disorder, substance-induced psychotic disorder, and psychotic disorder due to specified general medical condition. The subcategories are otherwise unchanged. Schizoaffective disorder is now classified with schizophrenia. It, by the way, is another concept that can be credited to Langfeldt (Maj, 1984). In general, however, this label is relatively unique to the United States. In many other countries, whenever any delusional or other florid symptoms are present, the diagnosis of schizophrenia is made. Conceptually, schizoaffective disorder is a hybrid of schizophrenia and the former manic-depressive disorders (now called bipolar), since the classical description of a schizophrenic includes the lack of affect or emotion.

At the beginning of this section, I commented on the state of hospital diagnosis in the early 1960s when I received my training. In the 1990s the diagnosis of schizophrenia in one form or another is no longer as predominant as it was. Among hospitalized patients in several different settings in which I now consult, this diagnosis vies with schizoaffective disorder and some type of bipolar diagnosis in popularity. This is neither a new nor a local phenomenon.

A study done by Blum in 1978 documented a shift between 1954 and 1974 that he suggested could be related to shifts in the patient population as well as changes in diagnostic categories. Several writers have commented on the changes. Ellard (1987) pointed out that one no longer sees patients who exhibit the immobility of catatonia. Voices, he felt too, were formerly more often located in the environment but now reside more within the patient's head when they occur. He searched the literature for historic accounts. Affective disorders seem always to have been with us, he found, but he could not definitively identify what he could label schizophrenia before the eighteenth century. He concluded that if the equivalent of a schizophrenia epidemic began in the 1800s, it is now apparently beginning to subside. Ellard himself was struck by the oddity of what he was suggesting, but he is not totally alone. Torrey (1980) concluded that schizophrenia increased during this century, suggesting that industrialization played some part in this. His view has received some support from information gathered by the World Health Organization (Cooper & Sartorius, 1977). Boyle (1990) suggested the diagnosis of schizophrenia may be declining in part because it formerly was confused with neurological disorders, particularly postencephalitic parkinsonism.

It is clear, however, that the result of a narrower schizophrenia category in the United States has been a greater number of diagnoses of it in males than females (Lewine, Burbach, & Meltzer, 1984; Westermeyer & Harrow, 1984). A more chronic course, less affect, and poorer premorbid level of functioning are now some of the requirements for the diagnosis of schizophrenia, and these seem to characterize more males than females. Women are diagnosed schizophrenic at later ages than men, and in general they have a better prognosis. They also have less of the so-called negative or deficit symptoms. Ring et al. (1991) suggested that males have a greater biological vulnerability to physical developmental abnormalities that increase their risk and worsen their prognosis.

Before ending discussion of general schizophrenia, mention must be made of the traditional approaches to this disorder in the professional literature until the present reemphasis on biological factors as its most probable etiological basis. The exploration of parent-child interaction prompted by psychoanalysis focused primarily on poor parenting by the mother. For a number of years, the schizophrenogenic mother held center stage. Gregory Bateson led the way by postulating the double-bind theory, which described the mother's behavior as inviting emotional response and then punishing the child for succumbing to the wish for emotional connection (Bateson, Jackson, Haley, & Weakland, 1956). This, he said, was the basis for schizophrenia. As a result, of course, women's mothering of their children was always suspect in such cases.

Many now question whether schizophrenia is one disease entity or a combination of vulnerability factors, some genetic and some environmental, that may combine in different ways in different cases (Greenwald, 1992).

Personality Disorders

Affect as a symptom is one of the determinants of mood disorders and, lo and behold, more women are diagnosed as depressed. In addition, many "schizophrenic" women have found themselves rediagnosed as having personality disorders, particularly the borderline personality disorder.

Some of the greatest conceptual changes have recently taken place in this category. The paradigm shift occurred with the publication of *DSM-III*. Before 1980, the personality disorders occupied a section in the manuals coequal with other labels. In the *DSM-I*, they were described as being

> characterized by developmental defects or pathological trends in the personality structure, with minimal subjective anxiety, and little or no sense of distress. In most instances, the disorder is manifested by a lifelong pattern of action or behavior, rather than by mental or emotional symptoms. (American Psychiatric Association, 1952, p. 34)

The overall category was subdivided into personality pattern disturbances, personality trait disturbances, sociopathic personality disturbances, and special symptom reactions. The first section included inadequate personality, schizoid personality, cyclothymic personality, and paranoid personality. The trait disturbances included emotionally unstable personality, passive–aggressive personality, and compulsive personality. The sociopathic personality disorders included antisocial reaction, dyssocial reaction, sexual deviation, and addiction. It was this subtype that probably best typified the general description of the category. A category called Special Symptom Reactions was also included, listing transient situational personality disturbance, gross stress reaction, and the adjustment reactions of childhood, adolescence, and late life.

In *DSM-II*, the general category was personality disorders and certain other nonpsychotic mental disorders. The subcategories of personality disorder were paranoid, cyclothymic, schizoid, explosive, obsessive–compulsive, hysterical, asthenic, antisocial, passive–aggressive, and inadequate. The other categories were sexual deviations, which included nine specifications including homosexuality, alcoholism, and drug dependence, with the subcategories specifying the drug of choice. Transient situational disturbances were given their own separate section. Homosexuality became sexual orientation disturbance in 1973 and was now reserved for those individuals "who are either disturbed by, in conflict with, or wish to change their sexual orientation" (American Psychiatric Association, 1974, p. 44). Homosexuality alone no longer merited a diagnosis, a change that came about, as previously described, after much political infighting.

As part of the multiaxial concept, axis II was introduced in *DSM-III* to code aspects of the person's long-term functioning. As previously noted, it was designed to indicate the presence of longstanding characterological patterns. Its use has continued through *DSM-III-R* to *DSM-IV*. For adults, the personality disorders are now coded on axis II in addition to or instead of symptom diagnoses, which are to be coded on axis I. In children, various developmental disorders are coded on axis II. The concept behind the two axes was never fully explained in any of the *DSMs*, and their use has some logical flaws. This will be discussed later.

In *DSM-III*, the specific personality disorders named are paranoid, schizoid, schizotypal, histrionic, narcissistic, antisocial, borderline, avoidant, dependent, compulsive, passive–aggressive, and atypical or mixed. *DSM-III-R* grouped these same disorders into clusters, but except for atypical, now named "personality disorder not otherwise specified," the list was not changed. *DSM-IV* now eliminates passive–aggressive personality, but the listing otherwise remains the same as before. Please see chapter 2 for the controversy that erupted during the preparation of *DSM-III-R* over the proposed addition of masochistic (or self-defeating) personality and other diagnoses.

As Widiger (1993) has pointed out, there was no empirical basis to distinguish among the different personality disorder diagnoses both in *DSM-III* and *DSM-III-R*. The number of criteria to be met, according to each definition, was set on the basis of agreement by the advisory committee. This apparently continued to be the procedure for *DSM-IV*.

Frances and Widiger (1986) have indicated both that "there is in fact very little available data to support the validity of most of the Axis II diagnoses, and virtually no data to support the theoretical speculations regarding specific etiology and treatment" (p. 382). Blashfield and Breen (1989) found that the categories listed in *DSM-III-R* had poor face validity and that the criteria for several supposedly different disorders overlapped considerably. Spitzer, Williams, Kass, and Davies (1989) also found it difficult to affirm meaningful distinctions between various personality disorders in a national field study.

The borderline personality disorder is the most problematical, especially as a diagnosis for women. The original concept for the label, now essentially forgotten, was that these people existed along the border between psychosis and neurosis. Occasionally they moved across the line but returned quickly to the neurotic side. Before *DSM-III*, a variety of labels were used for this disorder, including pseudoneurotic schizophrenia (Hoch & Polatin, 1949) and latent or incipient schizophrenia. The current view of BPD is quite different and often focuses on the difficulties of helping these women, who are quite emotional and react unpredictably to persons who try to work with them. Despite the title, they are no longer conceptualized as being on the borderline between neurosis and psychosis.

Although abuse history is not yet routinely asked for (and some severely disturbed persons may not be able to report it even though it exists), recent studies have discovered that a high percentage of hospitalized psychiatric patients have been abused (Carmen, Reiker, & Mills, 1984). A recent study (Bryer, Nelson, Miller, & Krol, 1987) found that nearly three quarters of 66 female patients had been physically and/or sexually abused at some time in their lives—a figure even higher than previously reported. In addition, the authors found that abused patients "have more severe and possibly psychotic or psychotic-like acute symptoms; they have more borderline diagnoses and character features; they have more suici-

dal symptoms; and finally, they are given pharmacological treatment more often" (p. 1429).

Whether individuals with a history of abuse are diagnosed primarily on the basis of their symptoms or on an etiological basis
related to their history is a theoretical matter, but it has profound
therapeutic and social implications. The personality disorder label
is one of the most stigmatizing that exists. It places traumatized
women struggling to survive in a hostile world in a tight pigeon-
hole that makes them different from everyone else. When abuse
history is not considered, those with this label (mostly women) are
seen as different from examiners, as often making examiners' or
therapists' lives difficult when they attempt to intervene, and in
general as unlikable and obnoxious. When practitioners recognize
that these women are reacting to traumatic histories, however, they
can see these women as distressed and attempting to cope with
their experiences. The patients and their symptoms can be placed
along an abuse continuum that could even include abuse experienced in the lives of their helpers. They thus become more human
and more understandable and are more likely to be helped and to
take that help in. Feminist clinicians, including this author, have
suggested that this is likely to be more therapeutic in the long run
(Herman, 1992a; Lerman, 1989).

The diagnosis of dependent personality disorder is also significant for women. The *DSM-IV* indicates, without supporting data,
that women do not receive this diagnosis more frequently than do
men. Bornstein (1996), after reviewing the literature on this matter,
indicates that the evidence does not uphold this contention. He
found that women receive this diagnosis at significantly higher
rates than men. After reviewing various hypotheses, he concluded
that the difference seemed to lay in women's greater willingness to
acknowledge dependency in response to interviews, rather than in
sex differences in dependency per se.

Posttraumatic Stress Disorder

The diagnostic category of posttraumatic stress disorder (PTSD),
introduced officially in *DSM-III*, is markedly different from other
diagnoses in the *DSMs*. Along with the diagnosis of adjustment
disorder, which has been in the manuals since *DSM-I*, it specifically
accepts environmental factors as legitimate causes of psychological
distress and for the occurrence of symptomatology. It is thus one of
only a few disorders whose description is related explicitly to eti-

ology (Green, Lindy, & Grace, 1985). PTSD is listed with the anxiety disorders but is distinguished from other diagnoses in this group by a specific description of environmental causes.

Posttraumatic stress disorder was to be diagnosed in *DSM-III-R* on the basis of

> the development of characteristic symptoms following a psychologically distressing event that is outside the range of usual human experience (i.e., outside the range of such common experiences as simple bereavement, chronic illness, business losses, and marital conflict). The stressor producing this syndrome would be markedly distressing to almost anyone, and is usually experienced with intense fear, terror and helplessness. (American Psychiatric Association, 1987, p. 247)

The key to this diagnosis, then, was that the external stressor occurs "outside the range of usual human experience" and that it "would be markedly distressing to almost anyone." The description went on, however, to state that "some stressors frequently produce the disorder (e.g., torture) and others produce it only occasionally (e.g., car accidents)" (Ibid). Although PTSD can be usefully thought of as a normal reaction to abnormal circumstances, this was not originally stated in *DSM-III*. Both *DSM-III* and *DSM-III-R* indicated that preexisting psychopathology could create a predisposition for the development of PTSD, but only *DSM-III-R* added the sentence: "However, the disorder can develop in people without any such preexisting condition, particularly if the stressor is extreme" (American Psychiatric Association, 1987, p. 247).

The closest parallel in the *DSM-III*s and *DSM-IV* to PTSD is adjustment disorder, defined in *DSM-III-R* as "a maladaptive reaction to an identifiable psychosocial stressor, or stressors, that occurs within three months after the onset of the stressor" (American Psychiatric Association, 1987, p. 329), and in slightly more neutral language in *DSM-IV* as "the development of clinically significant emotional or behavioral symptoms in response to an identifiable psychosocial stressor or stressors" (American Psychiatric Association, 1994, p. 623). The stressors suggested here include the ordinary ones excluded from the PTSD category. The trauma could involve single or recurrent incidents, and can included individualized psychological reactions to events or natural disasters. It is also noted that "The severity of the reaction is not completely predictable from the intensity of the stressor" (American Psychiatric Association, 1987, p. 329). A crucial element in this diagnosis, however, is that the reactions are to occur within three months of the onset of the stressor and to persist for not more than six months. Generally, too, the symptom of traumatic flash-backs to the event(s) is not expected to be present. With the exception of the time constraints, the criteria for this diagnosis are more open and flexible than those for PTSD.

No diagnosis in *DSM-II* or earlier was comparable to PTSD, although transient situational disturbance is listed. Its difference from posttraumatic stress disorder can be noted, however, by its description, which obviously comes from a very different philosophical stance:

> This major category is reserved for more or less transient disorders of any severity (including those of psychotic proportions) that occur in individuals without any apparent underlying mental disorders and that represent an acute reaction to overwhelming environmental stress. A diagnosis in this category should specify the cause and manifestations of the disturbance as far as possible. If the patient has good adaptive capacity his [sic] symptoms usually recede as the stress diminishes. If, however, the symptoms persist after the stress is removed, the diagnosis of another mental disorder is indicated. (American Psychiatric Association, 1968, p. 48)

The original impetus for including posttraumatic stress disorder in the *DSM* came from veterans groups and those who worked with the aftermath of military service on young men (and some young women), especially after the Vietnam War. Although it had not been officially listed before, this diagnosis has a long history that predates World War I. Freud and others referred to railway psychosis, the aftermath of train disasters, and World War I popularized the term shell shock, generally referred to as combat fatigue in World War II. Abraham Kardiner wrote about traumatic neurosis early, and, as mentioned, Sigmund Freud differentiated between traumatic neurosis and psychoneurosis (Trimble, 1985).

In addition to its use with veterans, the diagnosis of posttraumatic stress disorder has increasingly been used since it was officially introduced for the private and individually experienced traumas women and children face. Clearly, however, the unusual experiences that caused it seem meant originally to have been limited to massive, widespread, publicly experienced catastrophes: earthquakes and other natural disasters, war, and war-based tragedies such as the Holocaust and displacement (Moses, 1978). Although the description of PTSD in *DSM-III-R* included the sentence: "The trauma may be experienced alone (e.g., rape or assault) or in the company of groups of people (e.g., military combat)," the bulk of examples are public disasters. Of course women, like men, can be victimized in public events, but the distinction between public and private often parallels that between "ordinary" and "extraordinary." It is apparently much easier to label public traumas or traumas experienced collectively "extraordinary." This reflects the patriarchal aspect of our world, where much of what happens to women is more likely to occur in the unseen, private, individual realm.

In *DSM-IV*, the term *extraordinary* is not used. Now,

> the essential feature of Posttraumatic Stress Disorder is the development of characteristic symptoms following exposure to an extreme traumatic stressor involving direct personal experience of an event that involves actual or threatened death or serious injury, or other threat to one's physical integrity; or witnessing an event that involves death, injury, or a threat to the physical integrity of another person; or learning about unexpected or violent death, serious harm, or threat of death or injury experience by a family member or other close associate. (American Psychiatric Association, 1994, p. 424)

None of the symptoms to be manifested has been changed appreciably. The new language is perhaps more neutral, but the threshold level for this diagnosis may turn out to be more difficult to reach despite the presence of equivalent symptoms as before. Many have argued that this category has been overused since it was introduced in 1980, especially for women. Now, instead of the subjectivity involved in defining *extraordinary*, those interested in women's mental health issues have to deal with the subjectivity involved in defining "threat." This, of course, has increasingly been a legal issue when women claim self-defense after killing a battering spouse, for example. Our criminal justice system considers it to be self-defense only if the threat was direct and immediate. A battered woman who kills her husband while he is sleeping because she fears for her life when he awakens has generally not had much success claiming self-defense in court. Feminist legal scholars have pointed out the inequity in this definition for women (Browne, 1987).

DSM-IV also for the first time includes a new category, acute

stress disorder, for symptoms that occur within one month of expo-
sure to an "extreme traumatic stressor" (American Psychiatric
Association, 1994, p. 429). This is a potentially useful addition, but
it also reflects the new criterion of life threat that has been set for
PTSD.

Feminists have been working hard to gain recognition for the
impact of the rape, incest, and battering traumas experienced by
women in private space. Such personal events, as their ability to
document them increasing shows, are actually so common as to be
disgustingly ordinary, however psychologically extraordinary they
may be in any particular woman's experience. A study by Burstein
(1985) indicated that "PTSD reactions can occur to a variety of stim-
uli" that are well within the ordinary or usual range, such as marital breakups and family deaths. More recently, Breslau and Davis
(1987) pointed out that there is little support for the *DSM-III* distinction between extraordinary and more ordinary stressors. They
indicate that "The likelihood of long-term psychopathological reactions is associated with preexisting personality characteristics or
with the nature of the social environment of the survivors" (Breslau & Davis, 1987). The battle between ordinary and extraordinary
has been at least temporarily won. How the concept of threat to life
will be used will determine the continued usefulness of this diagnostic label.

Feminists and others have increasingly called for attention to the
long-term psychological effects of sexist and female-abusing environments on women's internal experience of themselves. The place
in the diagnostic manual into which these concerns would best fit
has now been narrowed to the point where, despite the research
results, we have no convenient category to use when we wish to
demonstrate the pervasive, fundamental effects of environmental
and social stressors on individual women. Some feminist suggestions for a remedy will be discussed in the final chapter.

A category called DESNOS (diseases of extreme stress not otherwise specified), first used by Bessel van der Kolk, had been proposed as an addition to the classification. DESNOS would account
for the experience of survivors of prolonged, repeated trauma
rather than single events. Judith Herman advocated it under the
title complex PTSD. Surely the psyches of girls and boys subject to
repeated, prolonged abuse, whether verbal, physical, sexual, or
some combination of all three, are affected, and specific ways of
dealing with the world develop into long-term patterns. For Herman this phenomenon is characterized by enduring personality

changes and high risk for repeated harm, along with the possibility of misdiagnosis as a personality disorder. She wished to see a full spectrum of trauma disorders from brief reactions through PTSD to DESNOS (Herman, 1992a). Because the process is closed, we do not have any concrete explanation for why the *DSM-IV* committee rejected the proposal for DESNOS. We know that van der Kolk advocated its incorporation, but Davidson and Foa (1991) did not discuss the possibility of including it. Since they were part of the PTSD task force, we may assume that DESNOS had already been discarded for *DSM-IV* by 1991.

Despite controversy over its placement, PTSD began in the anxiety disorder section of *DSM-III* and has remained there through *DSM-IV*. From one simple category, anxiety reaction, listed as one of the subgroups under psychoneurotic disorders in *DSM-I* and holding similar status in *DSM-II*, the anxiety disorders grew to a separate group in *DSM-III* and the manuals since. *DSM-IV* contains separate categories for panic disorder with and without agoraphobia and agoraphobia without history of panic disorder, specific phobia, social phobia, posttraumatic stress disorder (discussed separately earlier), acute stress disorder, generalized anxiety disorder, anxiety disorder due to medical condition, substance-induced anxiety disorder, and the by now familiar "Not Otherwise Specified" (American Psychiatric Association, 1994).

The anxiety disorders are included here both for the sake of completeness of coverage and because they are most frequently diagnosed in women (Dick, Bland, & Newman, 1994). A highly specialized group of mental health practitioners have emerged who treat these disorders, usually with some form of behavioral therapy approach and possibly medication. Because the treatment procedures are specific, the danger arises that antecedent events in the person's life will not be fully enough explored to uncover prior social and familial trauma, relationships, and other contextual factors that may contribute to these symptoms.

Sexual Dysfunctions

DSM-I and *DSM-II* did not include a category for sexual dysfunctions. The only remotely related categories listed were sexual deviations listed under the headings Personality Disorders and Certain Other Non-Psychotic Mental Disorders. Sexual dysfunction was also not listed under special symptoms, a miscellaneous classification where it logically might have fit.

One must remember, of course, that Masters and Johnson's first book was published in 1968 and that their *Human Sexual Inadequacy* was not published until 1970. The entire field of sex therapy, which emerged only later, did not therefore exist when *DSM-II* was published in 1968. *DSM-III*, by contrast, included a section on psychosexual disorders with four subheadings: gender identity disorders, paraphilias, psychosexual dysfunctions, and other psychosexual disorders. Here, sexual dysfunctions had its own section and was not included (as in *DSM-II*) under personality disorders. What had been listed in *DSM-II* as sexual deviations were now classified as paraphilias. The rationale given for the switch in terminology was that "The term Paraphilia is preferable because it correctly emphasizes that the deviation (para) is in that to which the individual is attracted (philia)" (American Psychiatric Association, 1980, p. 267). This was one instance among others of a return to older Latin- and Greek-based terminology rather than relying on more current English usage. It suggests an increase, rather than a decrease, in the mystification and reification of classifications. Ego-dystonic homosexuality was now the label for one of the disorders under the heading Other Psychosexual Disorders. The only other listing, under the heading Psychosexual Disorder Not Elsewhere Classified, suggested that it could include the following:

> (1) Marked feelings of inadequacy related to self-imposed standards of masculinity or femininity, such as body habitus, size and shape of sex organs, or sexual performance; (2) impaired pleasure during the normal physiological pelvic responses of orgasm; (3) distress about a pattern of repeated sexual conquests with a succession of individuals who exist only as things to be used (Don Juanism and nymphomania); (4) confusion about preferred sexual orientation. (American Psychiatric Association, 1980, p. 283)

The *DSM-III* categories for sexual dysfunction included inhibited sexual desire, inhibited sexual excitement, inhibited female orgasm, inhibited male orgasm, premature ejaculation, functional dyspareunia, and atypical psychosexual dysfunction. The description of the latter stated: "An example would be no erotic sensations or even complete anesthesia despite normal physiological components of sexual excitement and orgasm. Another example would be a female analogue of Premature Ejaculation" (American Psychiatric Association, 1980, p. 281). The categories, of course, are roughly comparable to ones specified by Masters and Johnson (1970). Also, since Masters and Johnson's early research, work has been done on identifying low sexual desire, and this has been included as well.

Leonore Tiefer (1988) notes that "it is important to notice how oriented they [the present categories] are to mechanical and heterosexual intercourse. Sexual disorders are physical failures in the performance of heterosexual intercourse" (p. 9). Note that the classification calls them psychosexual dysfunctions but does not discuss the psychosexual aspects of the physical sexual behavioral states mentioned. The Campbell dictionary defines *psychosexual* as "Relating to sexuality as it manifests itself in the mind, in contradistinction to its physical or somatic manifestations" (Campbell, 1989, p. 509).

Let us compare *DSM-III-R* with *DSM-III*. First, the overall heading was now Sexual Disorders. Also, gender identity disorders had been moved out of the general category of sexual disorders and had now been placed under the heading Disorders Usually First Evident in Infancy, Childhood, or Adolescence. Some of the entries under the paraphilias had also been changed. Sexual dysfunctions had been subdivided into sexual desire disorders, sexual arousal disorders, orgasm disorders, sexual pain disorders, and "Not Otherwise Specified," although the actual categories remain roughly comparable to those in *DSM-III*. The only really new category was sexual aversion disorder. Impaired physiological pleasure (listed as example [2] in *DSM-III*) is omitted as one of the examples of the "Not Otherwise Specified" sexual disorder.

In *DSM-III*, the descriptions of inhibited female orgasm and inhibited male orgasm were not fully comparable. For the female, the description included the idea that the diagnosis could be made after "sexual activity that is judged by the clinician to be adequate in focus, intensity, and duration" (American Psychiatric Association, 1980, p. 279). For the male, though, the only requirement was "an adequate phase of sexual excitement" (ibid., p. 280). In *DSM-III-R*, the descriptions of hypoactive sexual desire disorder (a diagnosis meant for both sexes), inhibited female orgasm, and inhibited male orgasm all include statements about the clinician's need to judge the adequacy of sexual activity. Premature ejaculation remained a label more under the control of the male (as it also was in *DSM-III*) whose ejaculation comes "before the person wishes it" (American Psychiatric Association, 1987, p. 295).

Some sexism in the language used to describe male and female sexual disorders in *DSM-III-R* compared to *DSM-III* was cleaned up. Tiefer (1988), however, writes:

The inescapable conclusion . . . is that what is really important to women in sexual life has been neglected by those who are "officially" in charge of defining and describing norms for sexuality in favor of a nosology which focuses exclusively on physical performance elements. In fact, many of women's concerns about intimacy, negotiation, spontaneity, communication, remembering preferences, etc. are addressed in formal sex therapy and may even take up the bulk of the therapy time and work. But these complaints are usually addressed only because it seems that they need to be in order for the couple to regain their ability to perform the normal intercourse-oriented sexual response cycle. (p. 16)

Her conclusion is also worth quoting:

Soble (1987) has recently discussed how the medicalized construction of sexual problems exclusively as performance difficulties, i.e., "machines in disrepair," fits nicely into familiar contemporary metaphors. The machine is rubbed, but it won't get hard, or won't get wet, or won't come. It's obviously in need of fixing/treatment. "It," the part, is not behaving in its "natural" way, as nature designed for it to behave, and as it would behave if there were not some obstacle in its way. This "essentialist" assumption, that there is some prior natural sexuality underneath all the culture, all the individual learning, all the social and religious values, is the root support for the DSM-III's authority and the authority of any medicalized model. By rejecting essentialist claims for sexuality, as we have for so many other aspects of life, feminists will seize the initiative to define and create a better world. As we've said all along, "The personal is political." Don't forget it. (p. 19)

Her points are still valid for *DSM-IV*.

Sexual Orientation

In the seventh printing of *DSM-II* in 1974, the definition of homosexuality as a psychiatric disorder was changed so that the diagnosis of sexual orientation disorder would be made only if an individual was distressed by having homosexual feelings or actions. This change, made in response to action by gay rights groups during the previous three years, was bitterly opposed by the American Psychoanalytic Association, whose president wrote to the American Psychiatric Association's then president objecting (on the basis of psychoanalytic theory) to the use of discomfort as a criterion for assessing abnormality in this or any other diagnostic entity. The change was incorporated into the nomenclature before *DSM-III* was published in 1980.

Homosexuality was not specifically mentioned in the 1942 Standard Nomenclature. Based on social views of homosexuality at the time, it probably would have been diagnosed under the subtype of psychopathic personality indicating pathologic sexuality. In the War Department manual of 1945, a potential diagnosis under pathological personality type was sexual deviate. An identical designation appeared in the 1947 nomenclature of the Veterans Administration. At that time and since, known homosexuality was a reason for discharge from the armed forces, so there was little use for a specific psychiatric diagnosis for it. In the original *DSM*, sexual deviation was a subcategory of sociopathic personality disturbance. This diagnosis directed specification of "homosexuality, transvestism, pedophilia, fetishism and sexual sadism (including rape, sexual assault, mutilation)."

In *DSM-II*, sexual deviations were listed separately under the heading Personality Disorders and Certain Other Non-Psychotic Mental Disorders. Homosexuality is specified as one of the subtypes, along with fetishism, pedophilia, transvestitism, exhibitionism, voyeurism, sadism, masochism, and other sexual deviation. Apparently, social views had changed enough that it was no longer listed as a sociopathic personality disturbance. After 1974, homosexuality was specified separately as sexual orientation disturbance, but it remained in the sexual deviations section of *DSM-II*. It does not appear at all in *DSM-IV*.

Dissociative Disorders

This is another category that has evolved from a single diagnosis, dissociative reaction, in *DSM-I* to a group of disorders in *DSM-IV*. Grouped here now are dissociative amnesia, dissociative fugue, dissociative identity disorder, depersonalization disorder, and dissociative disorder not otherwise specified. What is now called dissociative identity disorder was labeled multiple personality disorder in *DSM-III* and *DSM-III-R*. Hysterical neurosis in *DSM-II* could be diagnosed with a dissociative subtype, and depersonalization neurosis was also mentioned.

This is an important category for women because dissociative symptoms play a part in PTSD (and some have suggested that PTSD be placed among the dissociative disorders rather than with the anxiety disorders). Pierre Janet was the first who studied dissociation, and with the increased interest in responses to trauma, we have become more interested in his work again in recent years (van der Kolk & van der Hart, 1989). Everyone dissociates (i.e., daydreams), but the line between what is considered normal and what is not is unclear. The fact that humans can dissociate means, among other things, that some habitual actions can occur automatically (i.e., driving an automobile) and that we can concentrate single-mindedly on one task. It is likely that dissociation enables people to compartmentalize traumatic experiences so that they can continue to function in other aspects of their lives. I often tell clients with a traumatic history that their ability to dissociate helped them survive their abuse but that continuing to dissociate to the same degree when the need to do so has passed is no longer functional in their lives.

Although multiple personality itself has a history going back to antiquity (North, Ryall, Ricci, & Wetzel, 1993), it was a rarely used diagnostic label until recently. It seems to occur—or to be diagnosed—at a much greater rate in the United States than anywhere else in the world (Atchison & McFarlane, 1994). The mental health field is in dispute over just how common it is. At the end of the nineteenth century a flurry of cases were diagnosed, but then the diagnosis seemed to go out of fashion until the 1950s. Today, it is generally perceived to be related to extreme physical and/or sexual trauma early in life. The use of hypnosis by therapists is also closely associated with this diagnosis. When it is diagnosed, it is diagnosed more often in females than in males. Some practitioners do not believe it exists, while others specialize in this disorder and tend to give the label to almost everyone they see. North et al. (1993) suggested that it is often difficult to differentiate from somatization disorders. It is also difficult to differentiate for some patients from borderline personality disorder and sometimes even schizophrenia. After their review of the literature, North and her colleagues concluded that MPD does exist but did not reach any firm conclusion about whether it is a distinct syndrome or exists only along with other disorders. They suggest that research be done on exclusion criteria, familial transmission, and controlled treatment studies, and that follow-up studies be conducted to determine its natural course.

Disorders of Childhood and Adolescence

Because few psychiatrists worked with children and young people when *DSM-I* was published and because psychiatric diagnosis was originally conceptualized for adults, *DSM-I* contained no separate diagnoses for children with the possible exception of what then was called mental deficiency. *DSM-II* included a section on behavior disorders of childhood and adolescence, which contained several reactions: hyperkinetic, withdrawing, overanxious, runaway, unsocialized aggressive, group delinquent, and others.

DSM-III reflected a drastic shift in how childhood disorders were labeled. It subdivided "Disorders Usually First Evident in Infancy, Childhood or Adolescence" into mental retardation, attention deficit disorders, conduct disorders, "others," eating disorders, stereotyped movement disorders, other disorders with physical manifestations, and pervasive developmental disorders. Specific developmental disorders such as reading, arithmetic, language, articulation, mixed specific, and atypical specific developmental disorders were to be coded on axis II (American Psychiatric Association, 1980).

In *DSM-III-R*, the major categories on axis I were disruptive behavior disorders, anxiety disorders, eating disorders, gender identity disorders, tic disorders, elimination disorders, speech disorders, and "others." The mental retardation categories were now to be coded on axis II along with the specific developmental disorders (so coded in *DSM-III*) and the pervasive developmental disorders (which include autistic disorder) (American Psychiatric Association, 1987).

In *DSM-IV*, mental retardation alone is coded on axis II, with the other categories moved back again to axis I. Other childhood disorders now include learning disorders, motor skills disorders, communication disorders, pervasive developmental disorders, attention-deficit and disruptive behavior disorders, feeding and eating disorders, tic disorders, elimination disorders, and others (American Psychiatric Association, 1994).

That there seems to be continuing vacillation about what disorders belong on axis II seems to me to represent both probable confusion about the meaning of axis II and lack of clarity about disorders specific to children. These disorders are not nearly as well conceptualized as adult disorders are. We will discuss issues related to axis II specifically later. Controversy has also arisen over the relationship between disorders diagnosed in childhood and later psychiatric disorders in adult life (Sroufe & Rutter, 1984).

Eating Disorders

When this category was first introduced, it appeared under the heading Disorders First Apparent in Childhood and Adolescence

(American Psychiatric Association, 1980). In *DSM-IV*, it appears as a separate grouping among the adult categories. It is a significant group of disorders because it appears predominantly in young women and its incidence appears to be on the increase (Strober, 1986). Since anorexia nervosa is based on a refusal to eat, it is relatively easy to diagnose whatever its etiology because marked weight loss cannot be disguised for very long. At its worst, it can be a life-threatening ailment. It has been viewed variously as an affective disorder, a compulsion neurosis, and an early form of schizophrenia. Where bulimia, or vomiting to purge food, is added to the picture, it is generally considered to be more complicated and difficult for the clinician to learn about and therefore to diagnose. There is a fine line between what is considered the normal dieting behavior among women in our culture and a severe disorder (Kaschak, 1992).

The problem is less with the diagnostic label than with different explanations of etiology, approaches to treatment, and the reasons for the current prevalence of eating disorders. They have definitely been related to sexual trauma (Everill & Waller, 1995; Mallinckrodt, McCreary, & Robertson, 1995), and it is also likely to be related to the other traumas women are generally subject to, which will be discussed later. Rothblum (1990), however, in discussing the myths about women and weight that predominate even in our current professional literature, pointed out that society's preoccupation with thinness, especially in women, is historically anomalous, a fad dominant only within the past 50 years. Because of the extent of professional mythologizing about the subject, including the view (demonstrated by Rothblum not to be true) that dieting is an effective way to lose weight, some of the problems that arise with it can be laid directly at the feet of the medical community itself.

Other Conditions That May Be a Focus of Clinical Attention

This category has been an issue since the publication of *DSM-III*. *DSM-I* included a category called Nondiagnostic Terms for Hospital Record. It included alcoholic intoxication (simple drunkenness), boarder, dead on admission, diagnosis deferred, disease none, examination only, experiment only, malingerer, and observation and tests only (American Psychiatric Association, 1952, p. 8). Except for intoxication, these were purely administrative categories. In *DSM-II*, an additional category was added, called "Conditions Without Manifest Psychiatric Disorder and Non-Specific Conditions" (American Psychiatric Association, 1968, p. 12). It included social maladjustments without manifest psychiatric disorder, marital maladjustment, social maladjustment, occupational maladjustment, dyssocial behavior, other social maladjustment, nonspecific conditions, and "no mental disorder" as its subcategories. This change began the trend that led to the present form of diagnostic terminology.

With *DSM-III*, what came to be called the V codes became a major and sometimes controversial issue. The category heading in both *DSM-III* and *DSM-III-R* was "V Codes for Conditions Not Attributable to a Mental Disorder That Are a Focus of Attention of Treatment." The section is even broader in *DSM-IV* and is broken down into relational problems, problems related to abuse or neglect (new), additional conditions that may be a focus of clinical attention, and additional codes. All of these are coded with numbers preceded by a V. The code indicates that no medical disease is involved but that treatment might be instituted.

Many have pointed out that the *DSM* now includes many common problems in living and question whether including them is appropriate because doing so essentially is based on a medical model of mental illness. While psychiatrists may treat such difficulties as noncompliance with treatment, bereavement, and problems with parent-child relations, school, occupation, identity, religion or spirituality, acculturation, and phase-of-life, it is more likely that other mental health workers such as psychologists, social workers, and pastoral counselors will deal with them. Insurance companies often do not pay for V code diagnoses, a fact that compounds the problem of falsification of diagnosis, which is discussed elsewhere.

Besides the V code diagnoses, *DSM-IV* also lists three other subcategories under this broad heading: psychological factors affecting medical condition, medication-induced movement disorders, and other medication-induced disorder. For the first, the diagnostician is to list the general medical condition and may choose among various factors that affect it, including mental disorder, psychological symptoms, personality traits or coping style, maladaptive health behaviors, and stress-related physiological response. These represent an expansion of what was a single classification of "Psychological Factors Affecting Physical Condition" in *DSM-III*. I suspect that the rationale for changing "physical condition" to "medical condition" may be psychiatrists' political need to emphasize that these new categories are more appropriately treated by them than by other mental health practitioners. The inclusion of medication-induced disorders is an attempt to deal with the major side effects of psychiatric medication (Cohen, 1994), although it is only a token measure at this time.

Organic Disorders

The scope and specificity of this category has greatly increased from *DSM-I* to the present, although it no longer exists under this general heading. Since the diagnosis of organic difficulties is generally made on a much more objective basis than the other diagnostic categories (although it may still often be difficult to differentiate from a functional diagnosis), it is not particularly important to discuss the specific categories here except to note that we know a great deal more about brain functioning than we did in 1954. Street drugs and their effects have also become more prominent since then. Present-day diagnosis often specifies the particular substance involved (if known) or the cause (trauma, vascular problem, etc.). We also have separate categories today for disorders related to caffeine and nicotine use. The general category now includes delirium, dementia, amnestic and other cognitive disorders, mental disorders due to a general medical condition, and substance-related disorders.

Other Categories Associated with Women

Hysteria

It would be odd to deal with diagnoses given to women without discussing hysteria, probably the prototypical diagnosis associated with them. As previously mentioned, the name originated with the Greeks, who assumed that the symptoms were due to the womb wandering from its assigned place if it was reproductively unfulfilled. Freud's earliest psychiatric work dealt with hysteria. After studying it in Paris with Charcot and in his own patients, he announced that it was due to "premature sexual experience occurrences which belong to the earliest years of childhood" (Freud, 1896/1962, p. 203). Later, after he abandoned the seduction theory as the basis of neurosis, he came to see hysteria as related to women's need to repress their formerly male sexuality at puberty (Lerman, 1986).

My first job after getting my degree in 1966 was at Topeka State

Hospital. Affiliated with the Menninger Clinic, the atmosphere was permeated with psychoanalytic thinking. Diagnosis was an important process that took weeks and culminated in a formal case presentation for each patient. A theoretical disputation at one of these comes to mind. A serious discussion took place over whether a woman could be designated as hysterical, regardless of other symptomatology, if she reported that she experienced orgasm during sexual relations. At a less formal level, I sometimes heard male therapists and diagnosticians seriously offer one sure sign that a given woman patient should be diagnosed as hysterical: that the male examiner became physically aroused in her presence. This is an aspect of diagnosis that has never been formally captured by the *DSMs*.

In the late 1960s women were still labeled frigid rather than nonorgasmic or preorgasmic. These latter terms demonstrate the strong possibility of change, something not acknowledged prior to the advent of sex therapy. Frigidity was considered to be one of the primary symptoms of hysteria. According to psychoanalytic theory, it occurred because of a woman's rejection of her true feminine sexuality (Lerman, 1986). Psychodynamic therapy of some type was generally advocated for this symptom even though it rarely resulted in any change in this supposed symptom of psychosexual disturbance. Other symptoms of hysteria, formulated in equally judgmental language, included: egocentric, exhibitionistic, emotionally shallow and labile, sexually provocative yet fearful of sexuality, suggestive, and dependent (Berger, 1971).

The concept of hysteria has generated considerable interest since the advent of the women's movement. While psychoanalysis has shifted to consideration of early childhood or oral phenomena, feminists have focused on the degree to which hysterical behavior caricatures or exaggerates what has been considered to be normal femininity. Even eminent psychiatrists have recently come to discuss it in these terms (Chodoff, 1982).

Although Freud's concepts held much sway in the psychoanalytic community over the years, hysteria was not specifically listed in *DSM-I* by name, probably because of the *DSMs'* origins in hospital practice. Under psychoneurotic reactions, however, conversion reaction was one of the categories. Because *DSM-I* grew out of World War II diagnosis of mostly male soldiers and veterans, this category was generally recognized, at least in part, as a euphemism for hysteria so that it could be diagnosed in men. As *DSM-I* described them, psychoneurotic disorders were characterized by anxiety. In conversion reactions, the anxiety was seen as being converted into a bodily ailment (American Psychiatric Association, 1952).

DSM-II, however, did list hysterical neurosis with two types, conversion and dissociative. It was

> characterized by an involuntary psychogenic loss or disorder of function. Symptoms characteristically begin and end suddenly in emotionally charged situations and are symbolic of the underlying conflicts. (American Psychiatric Association, 1968, p. 39)

This characterization very much corresponds to the psychoanalytic interpretation of its meaning.

DSM-III did not use the term hysteria. Conversion disorder was now listed under anxiety disorders; dissociative disorders had a section of their own, and the category included psychogenic amnesia, psychogenic fugue, multiple personality, and depersonalization disorder. *DSM-III* also included a category of somatoform disorders. The introduction to this section stated that disorders formerly diagnosed as either hysteria or Briquet's syndrome now belonged in this category (American Psychiatric Association, 1980, p. 24). Histrionic personality disorder on axis II was another possible diagnosis, as was brief reactive psychosis.

In *DSM-IV*, conversion disorder is now listed under somatoform disorders. The anxiety disorders and the dissociative disorders remain, and a new category called factitious disorders, can also be related to what was once called hysteria. In addition, of course, histrionic personality disorder and brief reactive psychosis also remain.

The term hysteria remains in the public consciousness, however, even though it no longer appears directly in the *DSMs*. Most often, it is used now to refer to what someone regards as overly emotional behavior on the part of a woman. At least once, Johnnie Cochran, defense counsel in the O. J. Simpson trial, referred to lead prosecutor Marcia Clark as hysterical and was chastised by the judge for uttering a sexist remark.

Similarly, psychologists have been significantly more likely to diagnose women than men as having histrionic personality disorder on the basis of equal symptoms (Hamilton, Rothbart, & Dawes, 1986). Hysteria may no longer be diagnosable directly, but categories that are its heirs have been and still are used in fashions that parallel its original sexist definition.

In addition to bearing a particular stigma when applied to a woman, a diagnosis of hysteria (conversion) historically seems also to have increased the likelihood that she will receive less than adequate medical care. Many patients originally labeled hysterical were later discovered to have had serious medical diseases that were misdiagnosed (Leigh, Price, Ciarcia, & Mirassou, 1982). This reflects physicians' acknowledged unwillingness to take women's accounts of physical symptoms seriously, particularly when their sources may be difficult to ascertain. Often, they do not even try and, instead, pass the woman on to their psychiatric colleagues, claiming that they found no physical basis for her complaints when, in truth, they never looked for any. The problem of the misdiagnosis of the physical as psychological will be further discussed later.

Disorders Related to Female Physiology and Function

We have already discussed the attempt to list some aspects of premenstrual syndrome as a distinct psychiatric entity. We only need to emphasize here that, despite the lack of research evidence, the general population generally regards PMS as involving some sort of emotional dysfunction.

At various times, as we have noted, involutional melancholia, now discredited, was considered to be a separate and distinct psychiatric category. Postpartum psychosis also had its day, although never as a separate formal category. *DSM-IV* lists it as one of the possible contributing possibilities under bipolar I (manic) disorders.

DSM-I listed psychophysiologic genitourinary reactions, described as including "some types of menstrual disturbances, dysuria [author's note: painful or difficult urination], and so forth, in which emotional factors play a causative role" (American Psychiatric Association, 1952, p. 30). The category remained in *DSM-II*, albeit with a slightly broader range. It now included "disturbances in menstruation and micturition, dyspareunia [author's note: pain during sexual intercourse], and impotence in which emotional factors play a causative role" (American Psychiatric Association, 1968, p. 47). *DSM-III* eliminated all the psychophysiologic reactions as a separate category. Functional dyspareunia was moved to the section on psychosexual dysfunctions, where it has essentially remained through *DSM-III-R* to the present *DSM-IV*.

In their recent review of psychiatric disorders related to female physiological processes, Gitlin and Pasnau (1989) concluded:

Psychiatric syndromes linked to reproductive function in women require continued interest and investigation. As post-hysterectomy depression and involutional melancholia fade into psychiatric history, we find that hysterectomy does not generally produce psychiatric damage and the involutional period is not associated with greater vulnerability to major depression. Postpartum illnesses seem destined to stay with us as consistent clinical entities, but postpartum psychosis is most likely a variant of primary affective illnesses and not a separate disorder. The single most important risk factor is a past psychiatric history, especially of affective illness. Research into PMS will expand as our methodologies improve. (p. 1420)

I have had occasion to discuss with other feminist therapists the impression that many of us have that women who have experienced sexual abuse (especially early in life) seem most likely to experience severe menstrual and sexual difficulties, apart from whatever broader psychological dysfunctions they manifest. Data have not yet confirmed this impression, and we certainly do not know to what extent severe menstrual difficulties may result from undiagnosed internal physiological injury existing alongside the sequelae of psychological trauma. The closest we have come are findings such as those of Walker, Gelfand, Gelfand, Koss, and Katon (1995), which demonstrated that, along with more psychiatric disorders throughout their lives, women with severe sexual abuse histories had a high number of unexplained medical symptoms. Golding (1996) also found recently that, in a sample of 3,419 women, physically violent assaults and those committed by strangers were strongly related to reproductive symptoms, whereas multiple assaults and sexual assaults by intimates were strongly related to the presence of sexual symptoms.

One side note to the present political furor over abortion is that the antiabortion side has suggested a postabortion disorder, despite evidence to the contrary (Russo & Zierk, 1992). It is not likely to make it into a *DSM* anytime soon, but it exists in the public consciousness.

Body Dysmorphic Disorder

This is a category originally introduced in *DSM-III-R* and maintained in *DSM-IV* in the section on somatoform disorders. Its essential feature is a preoccupation with a defect in appearance or physical anomaly that may be either imagined or exaggerated. Any body part may be the focus of concern, including, of course, the genitals or breasts. *DSM-IV* indicates that "preliminary evidence suggests that Body Dysmorphic Disorder is diagnosed with approximately equal frequency in women and in men" (American Psychiatric Association, 1994, p. 467).

Although I have had male clients who do not believe their physique is sufficiently muscular, their penises large enough, or who think they look too feminine, I find the statement about the gender ratio in this category difficult to accept and await its independent validation or refutation. Practically no woman I have ever met, whether socially, as a colleague, or professionally, believes (without a great deal of psychotherapeutic work) that her body is adequate. In the consciousness-raising group for women professionals through which I started on my own professional (and personal) road to feminism, not one woman considered her breasts to be the right size. In all instances, they were either too small or too large. This disparagement of physical appearance also extended to other parts of their bodies. Iris Fodor (1996) has provided an excellent description of how women internalize sociocultural messages as shame about body issues. In 1993 Cash and Henry (1995) repeated a nationally representative survey originally done in 1985 and found that women's global body-image evaluations have worsened during this interval. Currently, nearly half negatively evaluated their looks and expressed concerns about being or becoming overweight, although black women had more positive body images than Anglo or Hispanic women. How many of these women would meet these three diagnostic criteria for body dysmorphic disorder in *DSM-IV*?

> A. Preoccupation with an imagined defect in appearance. If a slight physical anomaly is present, the person's concern is markedly excessive.
>
> B. The preoccupation causes clinically significant distress or impairment in social, occupational, or other important areas of functioning.
>
> C. The preoccupation is not better accounted for by another mental disorder (e.g., dissatisfaction with body shape and size in Anorexia Nervosa). (American Psychiatric Association, 1994, p. 468)

Few women look like the women who commonly appear on TV or in the movies and are touted as ideal. The disparity affects most women profoundly early in life and may well contribute to an increase in eating disorders and the difficulty in being able to clearly distinguish between disorders and the "normal" female dieting and other behaviors that Ellyn Kaschak (1992) has described so well. The description of body dysmorphic disorder explicitly indicates that it is not to be diagnosed when an eating disorder is diagnosed. Cultural issues are mentioned briefly in its general description in *DSM-IV* but without specification. The description focuses on the concerns of the individual without relating it well to real social pressures. The line seems hard to draw between what unfortunately are culturally normative concerns about appearance and this purported malady.

THEMES OVER TIME

Greater Inclusion

When comparing the various *DSMs*, one notices immediately that they have become progressively larger, both in format and content. *DSM-I* was 129 pages long and the pages were small, approximately 5 by 8 inches. *DSM-II* ran to 119 pages whose size was approximately 5¾ by 8¾ inches. The *DSMs* since have been in a larger book format measuring 7 by 10 inches. They have also each been considerably longer, running to 494 pages for *DSM-III*, 567 pages for *DSM-III-R*, and 886 pages for *DSM-IV*. The number of diagnostic categories included has also grown, as has the specificity of many of the classifications. *DSM-I* described approximately 79 different diagnostic categories; *DSM-II*, 158; *DSM-III*, 224; *DSM-III-R*, 255; and *DSM-IV*, 370.

If one considers that the social purposes served by the classification system have also altered considerably over time, the increase in size becomes at least somewhat understandable. The coalescence of diagnoses into systems originally began, as we have seen, simply in order to maintain an inventory of patients housed in asylums and mental hospitals. At that time, there was a clear-cut division between "them" and "us," between the crazy and the rest of us. This changed partially because of the influence of psychoanalysis, which saw psychological conflicts in all or most of us, and partially because of the military's specific needs in diagnosing and treating transient and traumatic reactions during World War II. For these reasons the system came to have much larger cultural significance as the idea permeated society that we could all suffer "mental" or emotional disorders.

More and more aspects of living have come to be included under the heading of psychopathology. This is especially significant for women. As Schur (1984) pointed out:

> Just about any female behavior which diverges from gender prescriptions is likely to be interpreted in mental illness terms. If a woman is too fat or too thin, if she is too aggressive or too passive, if she is an unmarried mother or voluntarily childless, if she is heterosexually "promiscuous" or living a lesbian lifestyle—some psychiatric theory will be put forward to "explain" the behavior or condition. This is patently *not* because of unintelligibility. There are perfectly good and "rational" reasons for all these behaviors and conditions. What seems to be happening instead is a compulsive *effort to find* a "basis" for imputing psychopathology. This is suggested particularly by the fact that *even in cases of women's victimization*, such imputation may occur. Examples would be psychological theorizing about why a woman "allowed herself" to be in a situation in which she was raped, or why a repeatedly battered wife could not "bring herself" to leave her husband [emphasis in original]. (p. 200)

With the exception of military personnel, at that time almost all men, women were the primary patients, especially initially. This is still true for outpatient psychotherapy (Olfson & Pincus, 1994). There are a myriad of possible reasons for this, ranging from reactions to the traditional restrictions on women's lives to society's acceptance of psychoanalysis's view that women were much less likely than men to achieve full (genital) psychological maturity (Lerman, 1986). Also it has been documented that women are more willing to admit difficulties and to explore the emotional aspects of life. The high degree of physical, sexual, and emotional trauma documented in women's lives is yet another factor.

From initially referring only to a small, specifically designated portion of the population, psychiatric labels have come to be used for all or most of us. In addition to the greater inclusion in the manuals of everyday issues that were formerly excluded, this trend can also be readily seen in the results of demographic studies that show that psychiatric labels have been attached to a large proportion of the populace. A recent one, for example, showed that 32% of American adults have at some time been diagnosed with a major psychiatric disorder (Robins, Locke, & Regier, 1991), although a large proportion of them never received treatment. The survey used most of the categories in *DSM-III*. In addition to the organic disorders,

Omitted disorders included posttraumatic stress syndrome, tobacco use, psychosexual dysfunction, transsexualism, ego-dys- tonic homosexuality, bulimia and pathological gambling. One dis- order assessed at all five of ECA [author's note: epidemiologic catchment area] sites, anorexia nervosa, is omitted because the number of cases identified was extremely small. (Leaf, Myers, & McEvoy, 1991)

An even more detailed survey (Kessler et al., 1994) used *DSM- III-R* categories but surveyed persons beginning at the age of 15. It omitted diagnoses known to have low prevalence and seems over- all to have included fewer categories. The diagnoses used included major depression, mania, dysthymia, panic disorder, agoraphobia, social phobia, simple phobia, generalized anxiety disorder, alcohol abuse, alcohol dependence, drug abuse, drug dependence, antiso- cial personality disorder, and nonaffective psychosis. This latter category was a summary category that included schizophrenia, schizophreniform disorder, schizoaffective disorder, delusional disorder, and atypical psychosis. In this survey, nearly 50% reported having a disorder during their lifetime and 30% reported at least one during the previous 12 months. The most common dis- orders were major depressive disorder, alcohol dependence, social phobia, and simple phobia. Fewer than 40% of those with a lifetime incidence and 20% of those with a recent disorder received treat- ment. Only 21% of all lifetime disorders occurred to persons hav- ing a lifetime history of only one disorder. The vast majority (79%) had more than one disorder (defined as comorbidity). More than half of all lifetime disorders occurred to the 14% who had a history of three or more disorders. This group also included the majority of persons with severe disorders.

Men were more likely to have substance use disorders and anti- social personality disorder than women, while women were more likely to have affective disorders (except for mania, for which there was no gender difference in this study) and anxiety disorders. This accords more or less with previous research. Contrary to the popu- lar view, however, blacks had a significantly lower prevalence of affective disorders and substance use disorders, a similar rate of the anxiety disorders, and no disorders in which their prevalence was higher than whites. Hispanics had a significantly higher prevalence of affective disorders in these results. Rates of almost all disorders declined with greater income levels and increased edu- cational achievement. The authors indicate that they do not know if there is a causal effect or if this finding is due to downward drift (i.e., illness causing movement to a lower class). Another reason might be the greater ability of those in higher socioeconomic levels to deliberately hide whatever treatment they receive from public scrutiny. Comorbidity was less likely within the previous 12 months in rural areas. Substance use disorders, antisocial personality disorder, and comorbidity were highest in the West. Anxiety disorders were highest in the Northeast. Almost all disorders were lowest in the South. Since this research did not use axis II diagnoses other than antisocial personality disorder, it provides no information on the prevalence and usage of these diagnoses. Neither this survey nor the one previously mentioned included PTSD, so the results need to be evaluated with that in mind.

Are we in the 1990s more psychiatrically ill than we were in the 1940s? One message to take from the increased number of psychiatric categories now available might be yes, if one takes this increase, as well as the results of such surveys as reported earlier, as representing some generalized objective truth. There is, of course, no way to directly answer the question, although attempts to address it have been made, mainly by describing the increased stresses of present-day living. Young and Erickson (1988) suggested, for example, not that traumas are more likely in our present culture but that in a time of much cultural shift and transition:

> individuals experiencing a traumatic event during psychohistorical dislocation are doubly affected. They are denied the cultural foundations which allow a strong, well-defined sense of self to develop, making them more susceptible to the development of PTSD. (p. 441)

In other words, it may be more difficult to recover from trauma now than was previously possible. We will discuss trauma more fully later in this chapter.

The answers to the question, of course, depend on one's perspective. It must be noted, however, that two distinct phenomena are at work. One is the possible increase in the percentages of persons experiencing mental illness; the other is the increased numbers who appear in the statistics because the number of categories has increased. These groups should not be lumped together. Greater inclusiveness apparently represents more a need for control of the mental illness arena by diagnosticians than it does any legitimate validated expansion for the criteria for mental illness and treatment.

That recent surveys have demonstrated that only about 30% of those diagnosed as having a mental disorder during their lifetimes have received treatment in and of itself raises questions about the meaning of dispensing such diagnoses. I doubt that the researchers would easily accept the idea that many so-called disorders are self-limiting and possibly even self-correcting. What, indeed, does it mean to receive a psychiatric label?

Greater Variety and Specification of Medications

From the early days when women received prescriptions of valerian drops or cocaine in tonics, they have been the primary consumers of prescribed mind-altering medications. Prather and Fidell (1975) demonstrated how in the early days of the present feminist movement psychiatric drugs were advertised differently to psychiatrists when they were intended to be used with women and with men. For men, the advertisements suggested that psychiatric drugs would help them recover from the immediate trauma of physical problems. Women, in contrast, were initially pictured as despondent, sitting in the midst of housecleaning materials (a mop and pail were typical), with the implication that medication would allow women to rise up and complete cleaning the house, which they had neglected during their depression. According to Linda Fidell (1981), the Federal Drug Administration reported in 1980 that over two thirds of prescriptions for psychotropic medications were given to women. In 1983, Cafferata, Kasper, and Bernstein found that "the likelihood of obtaining psychotropic drugs was generally higher among women than men, regardless of family role responsibilities, social support provided by family structure, or family stressors" (p. 138). More recently, Pitts (1995) found that in a large managed-care practice near Chicago, 81% of female clients compared to only 53% of male clients were prescribed medication. She suggested both that a greater proportion of long-term clients receive medication (and more of these are women) and that "Current psychopharmacology does not offer medications which ameliorate rage and violence, symptoms more typically manifested by males. However, there is easy access to effective antidepressants" (p. 4). Pitts also suggested that because women are generally more emotionally demonstrative, "a desire to comfort and relieve may drive a doctor to medicate a woman patient who is weeping and visibly upset" (p. 5).

My response to Pitts's first point is that major tranquilizers are used to alleviate rage and prevent violence, but primarily in inpatient settings. In my opinion, these drugs are not customarily prescribed for violence on an outpatient basis, nor has there been any impetus for drug companies (the primary researchers in this area) to develop additional drugs for such uses because society does not generally define male violence as a psychiatric problem. Her second point is also an important one and will be explored further when we discuss how diagnosis (and, by implication, treatment) is filtered through the authority and judgment of the examiner.

Although anxiety medication and antidepressives often work, medication can easily be misused. Linda Gray Sexton tells of disposing of huge jars and other caches of medications she and her sister found after the death of their mother, the poet Anne Sexton (Sexton, 1994, pp. 199–200), some of which she had used in suicide attempts. Physicians often fail to inquire about medications other physicians may have prescribed or deal well with the possibilities of addiction to prescribed medication. Much psychotropic medication is currently prescribed by nonpsychiatric physicians.

The current crop of antipsychotic medication is less sedative than earlier varieties. Despite claims made about them, however, I have rarely seen them actually work to alleviate delusional states and lessen illogical thinking, although in general the patient is more calm and less troublesome. Almost all the medications, however, have side effects, some of which are severe and some of which are permanent (Breggin, 1990, 1991).

Increased General Knowledge

Notable advances have occurred in the behavioral treatment of sexual disorders, phobias, and several other specific entities. Also, for some of the newly identified traumas—rape, incest, battery, and so forth—as well as for PTSD in general, some treatment programs have been proposed. Notwithstanding this, only perhaps in the special case of organic disorders can our new and specific categories truly be said to represent demonstrable progress in scientific knowledge about the brain and its functioning. Our knowledge here, although still minimal, has vastly grown. Since the time of *DSM-I*, too, society has become more open about the use and abuse of a larger variety of chemical substances. We have accumulated greater knowledge about how illegal drugs, prescribed medications, alcohol, and even everyday substances such as coffee, tobacco, and various foods affect psychological and physiological functioning. The organic section of the latest *DSM* thus in my view is the only section whose specificity can as yet reasonably be justified. The specificity of other sections could only be justified if, say, the treatment (whether psychotropic or psychotherapeutic) prescribed for subcategories of dysphoric disorder were different, which it decidedly is not.

Societal Changes

Our society has experienced many changes during the period of time we are discussing. Collectively, we have lived through the end of World War II, a cold war, the Korean War, a divisive war in Vietnam, a black civil rights movement, a renewed women's movement and more women moving into the workforce, a gay liberation movement, a hippie era, a humanistic psychology era in which it seemed that anything and everything could have therapeutic value, the assassination of John Kennedy and Martin Luther King, the birth of television leading to a mass media explosion that we couldn't have dreamed of previously, an electronic revolution in the home and office, an increasing chasm between the haves and the have-nots, and a new period of immigration, both legal and illegal, this time from Asia, Mexico, and Central and South America rather than Europe.

No one can possibly doubt that these events and many more have had some kind of impact on the form and nature of the *DSMs*, however much the claim is made that changes have been brought about purely by advances in scientific knowledge. We have already discussed the influence of gay and feminist activism in the dropping of homosexuality as a disorder from *DSM-II* and the reaction to the controversial diagnoses in *DSM-III-R*. Professional organizations such as the American Psychiatric Association, promulgator of the *DSMs*, whose members are primarily affluent white males, tend to be conservative. The specific effects of the monumental events of the past 50 years, therefore, probably cannot be directly identified, but they probably spurred at least minimal recognition of ethnic, racial, or sexual diversity in the diagnostic manuals.

Women's increased presence in the workforce has extended into psychiatry as it has into every other profession. Some women psychiatrists have been working in a variety of ways for change in organizational recognition both for themselves and their female clients, as have female psychologists and other mental health workers. To all of these, we owe the recognition that incest and other sexual abuse of women and girls is a significant problem, one that unfortunately is a mental health issue for women, something definitely not acknowledged in the 1940s. It was not until the 1970s that Freud's convenient view that girls always fantasized sexual relations with their male parents (and also male psychotherapists) was definitively disputed and women's claims began to be believed (Lerman, 1986). This has also been occurring for rape, domestic battery, and other forms of violence against women.

More Specific Knowledge About Women

The second women's movement over the last 25 years released an explosion of creative energy by and about women and has resulted in a great deal of specific new knowledge about women at both the physical and psychological levels. Women (primarily but not exclusively) have researched the hidden history of earlier women, identified aspects of women's lives such as physical and sexual abuse that were previously denied and ignored, explored stereotypes about women, and researched aspects of female physiology to which men previously showed indifference. As noted, comparatively little of this material has, to date, influenced *DSM-IV* except in superficial ways.

Part of this change has resulted from feminists' recognition that they dispute traditional (read male) formulations of scientific issues. (For a recent discussion on feminist research, see Worrell and Etaugh [1994] and Wood [1995].) As will be seen when alternatives are discussed, unless our professional society undergoes a paradigm shift from classification per se to a more contextual approach, it is unlikely that newer knowledge about the psychology of women will ever be fully captured within the traditional format of the official classification system.

In the early 1970s, when women first began to research what history (both general and professional) had allowed to be forgotten, the saying "Anonymous was a woman" became a shorthand reminder that throughout history, if a woman had ever said or written anything significant and if the material itself survived and was passed along, her name was not likely to be attached to it. This has been demonstrated in most areas of art, literature, and science. Women's rediscovered contributions often expressed ideas and viewpoints that now sound insightful and proposed solutions that, although still largely untried, sound eminently reasonable today to those who are predisposed to listen to them.

Until this point, we have focused largely on the official forms of diagnosis. Unofficial diagnosis of the type discussed in the section on early history has, of course, never ended. Some examples follow.

Female Sexuality

Identifying what had been forgotten, for example, Lunbeck studied the records of the Boston Psychopathic Hospital between 1912 and 1920. Five percent of all patients were labeled psychopathic; three quarters of these were women. This was a highly unusual (to say the least) use of that term. It was popularized by Richard von Krafft-Ebing (1902/1965) in *Psychopathia Sexualis,* who used it almost exclusively to designate what were then known as the sexual perversions (including homosexuality). His famous book is a compendium of brief case descriptions of various perversions. Although he mentioned women, the greatest number involved men. Before Krafft-Ebing and after him, the term psychopathic has been generally used to refer to behavior that is abnormally aggressive and/or seriously socially irresponsible (Campbell, 1989). At the beginning of our century, it generally included or had strongly implied sexual connotations as well. This was the sense in which Krafft-Ebing used the term.

As the rigid Victorian morality wherein women were generally seen as not having sexual desires gave way, the term psychopathic, previously applied to male deviants, was employed to classify what were seen as hypersexual psychopathic women.

> The significance of psychiatrists' interventions lies not in their success in controlling, or even defining, female sexuality, but in identifying and attempting to comprehend a social change of singular importance: the emergence of the independent, sexually assertive woman in American society at the turn of the century. (Lunbeck, 1987, p. 514)

Lunbeck additionally pointed out that

> the concern over female autonomy that was implicit in the category of hypersexuality helps explain why psychiatrists considered failure to engage in heterosexual courtship—whether simple lack of interest or overtly lesbian behavior—just as psychopathic as a woman's too vigorous exercise of her seductive powers. (p. 522)

In addition, class and racial issues were also elements in this phenomenon. The majority of the designated patients were young working-class women whose behavior was incomprehensible to the middle-class female social workers who dealt with them. The two views, originally related to class differences, clashed, and the middle-class establishment view of moral behavior was the norm against which young women's attempts at individuality and sexual choice were measured and found wanting. On the other hand, at the same time, stereotypes of black immorality were prevalent, and so sexually independent black women were considered normal and did not receive the psychopathic diagnosis given to white women unless their behavior was so extreme that "it offended even the low standards of their race" (Lunbeck, 1987, p. 536). In one sense, this could be seen as an early reaction to different racial definitions of behavior, but it was based on stereotypes rather than a realistic appraisal of differences in the cultural meanings of behavior.

By the 1920s, the diagnosis of hypersexuality faded away and the label of sexual psychopath was again given mainly to deviant males. The lesbian replaced the hypersexual as the epitome of deviant female sexuality in the minds of professionals and the public alike (Lunbeck, 1987). All of this occurred outside the realm of official diagnosis. Lunbeck saw the phenomenon she described as a reaction to a major change in women's roles that was just beginning to occur.

Other scholars have pointed out that the topic of women's sexuality and who defines it continues to be a prominent power issue in the relations between women and men throughout society (Schur, 1984). Some specific instances of how this struggle has entered into the descriptions of female sexual dysfunctions in the *DSMs* have already been described. We need to add here the concept of nymphomania, prevalent during the nineteenth century. Previously known as furor uterinus, at this time it acquired additional names as well: metromania, andromania, hysteromania, clitorimania, and lypatia (Ricci, 1945). Various suggested treatments included washing the genitals with herbal mixtures, internal administration of camphor, and sometimes excision of the clitoris. Others advocated an apparatus made of wire mesh that when worn prevented masturbation (Ricci, 1945).

In mental hospitals in the 1960s, one of the signs that staff saw as representing improvement in women patients was that they would begin to wear lipstick. Grooming, in the sense that goes beyond cleanliness, was taught to women patients. A sign of good mental health for women was that they showed a desire to appeal to the opposite sex. This shift was never directly reflected in the diagnostic manual, but was used as a diagnostic sign. Of course, it was not supposed to be overdone (as measured by male eyes), or the woman would be labeled wanton or a nymphomaniac or whatever the current term was for the other end of the continuum.

At the Topeka State Hospital where I worked, adolescent women were hospitalized when incest with a family member was discovered, while the male perpetrator might go to prison. Just as we have moved beyond the view that women's expression of sexuality and menstruation in and of itself represents mental disorder, we have now in the enlightened 1990s moved somewhat past the view that the fact of sexual abuse is sufficient to warrant some kind of diagnosis of the young woman, although this progress has not shown up in the diagnostic manuals either. However, except perhaps in the description of PTSD, not even the latest *DSM* explicitly recognizes many facts related to women's everyday traumas such as incest, rape, and battery, which have become well known and well accepted in the mental health field.

In addition to Lunbeck's work, all of this clearly points out again that diagnosis does not occur in a social vacuum, that diagnosticians exist in their own time, and that, like fish in water, they cannot identify the medium in which they operate. No doubt most people generally did what they thought was best from their narrow viewpoint, but they remained blinded by the social conventions of their day.

Sexual and Physical Abuse

My previous discussion of axis II personality disorders, particularly borderline personality disorder, mentioned examples from the growing body of literature illustrating that persons (usually women) hospitalized for psychiatric problems have abuse histories, regardless of their particular diagnosis (Bryer, Nelson, Miller, & Krol, 1987; Carmen, Reiker, & Mills, 1984). By now, there is no doubt that physical and sexual abuse of girls and women is related in complex ways to a wide variety of later psychiatric diagnoses. Beitchman et al. (1992), after reviewing the literature, concluded that, although it is an important problem, the specific effects of sexual abuse have not yet been separated from the force, threat of force, and family psychopathology that usually coexist with it.

Recently, sexual abuse has been correlated with depression (Hamilton & Jensvold, 1992) and eating disorders (Andrews, Valentine, & Valentine, 1995; Everill & Waller, 1995; Mallinckrodt, McCreary, & Robertson, 1995), somatization disorders (Morrison, 1989), and implicated also in psychotic disorders (Darves-Bornoz, Lemperiere, Degiovanni, & Gaillard, 1995). Self-definition as having been physically abused (usually involving a higher threshold than that used by objective raters) was related to depression, hospitalization history, suicide attempts, and self-injury (Carlin et al., 1994).

In the past two decades we have accumulated much evidence on the prevalence of sexual abuse in particular (Finkelhor, Hotaling, Lewis, & Smith, 1990). Our information about psychiatric patients usually comes from psychiatric files, although there are as yet no indications that this information is even systematically collected. In other words, any prevalence statistics formulated in this manner are extremely likely to underestimate prevalence (Randall, Josephson, Chowanec, & Thyer, 1994). In a survey of nonpatients Russell (1986) found that some type of sexual abuse was reported by 37% of the participant women. Gail Wyatt (1985) found that sexual abuse, which has apparently not abated within the past two decades, is of equal concern to black and white women.

We have also learned that, at least in the case of sexual abuse, society has over at least the last two centuries alternately remembered that it occurs a great deal and forgotten that it plays a part in women's reactions to living. I (Lerman, 1986), among others, have discussed how Freud discovered and then lost awareness of the meaning of sexual trauma in women's lives. Masson (1984) pointed out also how it had been known and forgotten before Freud. Enns, McNeilly, Corkery, and Gilbert (1995) point out how the Kinsey reports of the 1950s briefly resurrected our awareness although they did not focus on the effects on the victim. It has taken the current feminist movement to really demonstrate sexual trauma's existence to society as a whole. That its existence and prevalence are still problematic to society in general is clear. A good discussion of the present backlash (a topic beyond the scope of this book) can be found in Enns et al. (1995) and the related discussion papers (Briere, 1995; Brown, 1995; Courtois, 1995; Lindsay, 1995; and Loftus, Milo, & Paddock, 1995). These articles specifically discuss the professional controversy that is currently raging about the existence and extent of repressed memories of childhood abuse that might be elicited during psychotherapy.

Menstruation and Reproductive Organs

Surprising as it may now seem, at the beginning of the twentieth century the physiological and hormonal aspects of menstruation were not well understood. The relationship of menstruation to ovulation was debated professionally until well into our century (Speert, 1980). The timing of ovulation itself was subject to guesswork, with many physicians propagating the idea that fertility was greatest just before, during, and after menstrual flow (Speert, 1980). A number of simply outrageous theories were promulgated, some of which were not very different from the beliefs of the ancient Greeks: The moon caused women to menstruate, the fetus was formed from menstrual flow, menstruation was pathological and proved the inactivity and threatened atrophy of the uterus, nervous stimulation triggered menstruation, etc.

Although the relationship of menstruation to ovarian activity was first postulated in 1831, the first discussion of the idea that women menstruated because they had not conceived took place in the 1880s. During this period, some suggested that the menstrual period was brought about by the death of the ovum in the uterus. Another suggestion was that menstruation was a type of spontaneous abortion. W. Heape fully discussed the purpose of menstruation in somewhat modern terms in 1896 (Ricci, 1945).

Mary Putnam Jacobi explored important aspects of women's reproductive functions and how they were related to the menstrual cycle (Walter, 1977). She likened the situation of human females to the growth of new cells in plants and suggested that menstrual blood was the dissipation of nutriment stored against the possibility of pregnancy. She was a proponent of the wave theory of menstruation, which postulated a decrease and increase in bodily functions during the menstrual cycle (Jacobi, 1885).

Whether officially labeled hysteria or not, during this period almost all ailments that women suffered were considered to be related either to her menstrual cycle or her uterus. Extreme measures were advocated for relief of female mental disturbances. Earlier, oophorectomies were done to cure hysteria and castration advocated as a cure for nymphomania or "a psychosis evoked or maintained by pathological alterations of the sexual organs, and in a neurosis originating from the same source" (*JAMA*, 1986, p. 2680).

Ricci (1945) described research of the period that found gynecologic lesions ("A circumscribed area of pathologically altered tissue" according to Thomas [1993, p. 1098], but not further specified by Ricci) in 40 out of every 100 female inmates of the Maryland Hospital for the insane. Speert quoted George Engelmann's address to the American Gynecological Society in 1877: "A reflex relation exists between the sexual organs and the sensitive impressionable mind of woman . . . [Speert's ellipses] insanity may be dependent upon functional derangement, upon disease or malposition of the womb" (Speert, 1980, p. 49).

In general, women were considered to be disabled when they menstruated, and between the ages of 12 and 20 they had to choose between working their brains and developing their reproductive systems. Any mental (or physical) activity during menstrual flow was considered to be especially injurious. Overstimulation of the female brain was assumed to cause stunted growth, nervousness, headaches, neuralgias, difficult childbirth, hysteria, brain inflammation, and even insanity (Bullough & Voght, 1973). Every ailment a woman suffered, particularly nervous ailments, was related to her womb (Wood, 1973).

All of this, please remember, was part of the medical literature and not just in the popular press. At the time, women were just beginning to demand better educational opportunities and greater political equality. Medical statements such as these were taken for scientific fact even though they were primarily based on individual opinion and conjecture. Among other things, physicians challenged women's ability to withstand the hardships of higher education. Even the eminent psychologist G. Stanley Hall ignored statistical studies demonstrating no difference in health between college educated and noncollege women. He repeated all the old fears about educating women in *Adolescence*.

A few women like Leta Hollingworth and Clelia Mosher challenged his views with their research (Bullough & Voght, 1973), although for the most part their views were ignored. There always were divergent voices although they seem to have been generally ignored.

Mary Putnam Jacobi (1895/1925) suggested that:

It is in the increased attention paid to women, and especially in their new function as lucrative patients, scarcely imagined a hundred years ago, that we find explanation of much ill-health among women, freshly discovered to-day, but which always existed, and which is often due to conditions arising among men, and not therefore new. Shattered nervous systems are inherited by girls from the alcoholism of the fathers; gonorrhea contracted by wives from husbands; sterility due to licentiousness in which the innocent woman may have no share; enforced celibacy due to bad social arrangements; occasionally, though less and less frequently, childbirths too close together; certainly all these causes of ill-health to women have existed for centuries. I think the peculiarity of the present time is that now attention is being drawn to the special effects produced upon women by these general causes. (p. 482)

Dr. Jacobi maintained that the ailments of female students might be the result of "competition, haste, cramming, close confinement, long hours, and unhealthy sedentary habits rather than to the exertion of mastering school textbooks" (quoted in Truax, 1952, p. 180). Her paper, answering the question "Do women require mental and bodily rest during menstruation; and to what extent" won Harvard's prestigious Boylston Prize. She sent questionnaires to 1,000 women; 33% of her sample of 286 indicated that they experienced no pain, weakness, or health deterioration. The more educated experienced less pain. Moreover, she pointed out that statistics from other parts of the world showed that working-class women have always worked without resting during menstruation (Jacobi, 1886/1978).

Despite the growth of knowledge in the twentieth century, we have seen that involutional psychosis was an accepted diagnosis, and we are still fighting the war around a psychiatric diagnosis premised on premenstrual syndrome (whatever its current name).

King (1989) has suggested a parallel between the myriad of symptoms provided in the past for neurasthenia and the equally broad array of symptoms associated with premenstrual syndrome. He also suggests parallels that can be drawn between the types of treatments offered: polypharmacy (his term for the use of a wide variety of medications as treatment), diet (different in each era but in accord with the particular popular dietary ideas of the period), exercise now versus the use of massage then, as well as surgical therapies.

Most recently, Klonoff and Landrine (in press) suggest that seizure disorders, especially ones with significant prodromal stages, are readily misdiagnosable as mood disorders. Since seizures in women are correlated with menstruation, they comment that the prodromal stage is often misinterpreted as premenstrual syndrome. Obviously, the medicalization of women's physiological processes continues into our day.

Sexual Abuse by Physicians and Therapists

Another increasingly well accepted and documented source of trauma, that of abuse of women patients and clients by mental health practitioners and other respected authorities, now falls under the broad PTSD rubric but is not explicitly mentioned in the *DSMs* (Gonsiorek, 1995). Like incest, it has an ancient history. The Hippocratic oath contains the first prohibition:

> Whatever houses I may visit, I will come for the benefit of the sick, remaining free of all intentional injustice, of all mischief and in particular of sexual relations with both female and male persons, be they free or slaves. (Edelstein, 1943, p. 3)

It seems likely that it would not have occurred to Hippocrates to include this prohibition if he did not know of instances in which this principle had been violated. Mary Putnam Jacobi (1890) remarked on essentially the same phenomenon among hospitalized women in her request for "female physicians for insane women." Some instances are reasonably well known among Freud's early followers (Lerman, 1986) where psychoanalysts married patients and/or sexually exploited them, an abuse that continues despite increasingly severe penalties (Gonsiorek, 1995).

Much more could be said about this subject. The most thoughtful and thorough discussion of the kinds of issues involved here can be found in Schoener et al. (1989), while the present author has compiled an annotated bibliography of cases and literature on this subject (Lerman, 1990).

As with the example of Charlotte Perkins Gilman used earlier, we have women writers who, in telling about what has happened to them, give us insight into what happened as well to a myriad of other women whose voices we cannot hear. For a recent example, consider Linda Gray Sexton's memoir of her mother, Anne Sexton. She wrote about the furor caused when Dr. Martin Orne released audiotapes of her mother's sessions with him to her biographer (Middlebrook, 1991), while the American Psychiatric Association did not even investigate Dr. Frederick Duhl for his sexual relationship with Anne Sexton while she was his patient (Sexton, 1994, p. 281), even after it became general knowledge. Major issues in the mental health field remain unaddressed about the prevention, detection, regulation, prosecution, and treatment for the results of iatrogenic abuses that turn into disorders.

Misdiagnosis of the Physical as Psychiatric

In the discussion of hysteria in chapter 2, we referred to some early research that verified that women labeled as hysterics often had misdiagnosed medical problems (Leigh, Price, Ciarcia, & Mirassou, 1982). Unfortunately this is not the only instance of such a phenomenon.

I have observed clinically that as soon as a patient, particularly a female patient, receives a psychiatric diagnosis, every discomfort or symptom she later reports is almost automatically assumed to be of psychological rather than physical origin, without investigation of her actual physical condition (Hamilton, 1989). Sometimes it seems that it would not be too extreme to say that it is believed that female psychiatric patients in inpatient or other institutional settings can never catch a cold.

The problem of misdiagnosis goes beyond this, however. Hoffman (1982) and Hall, Popkin, Devaul, Faillace, and Stickney (1978) documented that many people receive psychiatric diagnoses in error when medical disorders are actually present. Unfortunately, neither article mentions the gender of the patient, although I suspect that a high proportion were female. Taylor (1990) indicated that the masquerade of physical conditions as psychological symptoms is quite common. He directed his attention primarily to organic mental disorders.

Fortunately, a current book (Klonoff & Landrine, in press) is devoted to the very problem of preventing the misdiagnosis of physical disorders as psychiatric in women. It focuses on the possibilities that endocrine and seizure disorders among others can manifest in ways that make them difficult to differentiate from anxiety, depression, and other psychiatric ailments, unless mental health personnel and medical practitioners look carefully. The authors make a revolutionary statement: *"The misdiagnosis of physical disorders as psychiatric in part accounts for women's higher rate of depression, anxiety and somatization disorders"* [emphasis in original] (ms. 24).

Summary

The views of the most well-established institutions have frequently lagged behind the rest of society. As demonstrated here and elsewhere, much that is regressive and not supported by data remains in the current *DSM*. Even when it is not directly stated there, many stereotyped, unscientific, male-oriented views about women remain in the practices of mental health practitioners today.

We have discussed the persistent tendencies to impute women's disorders to their reproductive organs and to control the expression of female sexuality. In addition to these, we have also, unhappily, had to report on society's ambivalent reactions to sexual and physical abuse, as well as the abuse of women patients by professionals. The fact that women's physical symptoms are not taken seriously, particularly when they bear a psychiatric label, has also been discussed.

CHANGES IN THE UNDERLYING THEORETICAL FRAMEWORK

The early *DSMs* were influenced by the ideas of biological causation espoused by Adolph Meyer, who called his views *psychobiology*. Although he wrote nearly 200 papers after he came to this country in 1892, Meyer left it to others to gather them in book form toward the end of his life (Lief, 1948). According to Meyer (1934/1948):

> Psychobiology is a frank and noncompromising formulation of "behavior with mentation" or ergasia, behavior integrated in a flow of economizing and yet amplifying system of signs or symbolization, constituting a specific set of facts and not only a special aspect, the mentally integrated functioning of the live human organism. (p. 594)

Meyer viewed his system as integrated and involving the whole person. He did include what we would consider social aspects of the human being insofar as he advocated that psychiatrists study sociology and philosophy, but he was adamant that physicians were better able to deal with the individual than psychologists, whom he saw as having a limited perspective. Although he generally referred favorably to the concepts of Freud and his followers, he seemed to view Freud's theoretical viewpoint as too narrow and the process of psychoanalytic treatment as overly time-consuming. In 1909 he spoke at the Clark symposium, which brought Freud and Jung to the United States, and was elected an honorary member of the New York Psychoanalytic Society when it was formed in 1911 (Lief, 1948, p. 231). Although Meyer used "man" with the global meaning of human, which was typical at the time, and did not differentiate in any way between male and female child and adolescent development, he frequently used "he and she" when referring to patients, a practice quite unusual for his time.

As evident in the discussions of hysteria, neurosis, and neurasthenia as well as in attempts to tie all aspects of women's mental functioning to their reproductive system, the view that mental disorder was biologically based was of long standing and predated Meyer. Skrabanek (1990) has described many of the physical cures for mental illness undertaken over the years, all of which presuppose biological causation. Prominent treatments at one time or another include bloodletting and transfusion, meodialysis, hallucinogenics, acupuncture, megavitamins, and various foods.

The next phase, initiated in large part by Freud, can really be said to be anomalous. That the mind influenced the body rather than the reverse was certainly one of the most revolutionary ideas that Freud formulated. Although acceptance of this view was initially slow, over time it eventually took hold with a vengeance and the pendulum swung from one extreme—that biology is all—to a view that not even Freud would recognize (remember "Anatomy is destiny" about women [Freud, 1924/1961]), although his theories definitely led toward that extreme and much of his own thinking focused in that direction. One clear example was his ready diagnosis of his patient Emma Eckstein's nasal bleeding following an operation on her nose by his friend Wilheim Fliess as hysterical and as expressing sexual longing. Eventually, it came to light that Fliess had left a gauze packet in her nose by mistake (Masson, 1984). The frequent misdiagnosis of the physical as psychological today may be traced back directly to the extreme pendulum swing initiated by Freud.

In the 1930s and 1940s, psychoanalytic thought first became a major organizing influence in American diagnostic formulations. Officially, it held this position until the 1970s, reaching its heyday in *DSM-II*. Psychoanalytic terminology still permeates the popular culture, and even in women's studies it has been especially influential in the areas of literature and history.

Laura Brown (1984) has pointed out that:

> The art, literature, and criticism of this century assume that there *is* an unconscious mind, that behavior *is* motivated and determined by early experiences, that there *is* an Oedipal struggle between father and son, that women *do* lack the objectivity

bestowed by a successful resolution of the Oedipal conflict. Having internalized psychoanalytic thought in so many and subtle ways, . . . many feminist therapists, indeed most literate members of Western Civilization, use psychoanalytic thinking as a standard against which the quality of other theories of human behavior can be measured [emphasis in original]. (p. 75)

The battle over the minimal use of psychoanalytic terms in *DSM-III* demonstrates the validity of Brown's point.

That the public and the media still think largely in psychoanalytic terms despite changes in the *DSM*s very likely also reflects the thinking of many mental health professionals, many of whom were trained in the heyday of psychoanalysis. In my previous book, I documented the problematic nature of psychoanalytic theory, even in its modernized form, for women's issues (Lerman, 1986).

The pendulum, however, has been swinging back toward organically based explanations of entities such as schizophrenia while the influence of psychoanalysis has also been waning (Bayer & Spitzer, 1985; Townsend & Martin, 1983). In *DSM-III* and *DSM-IV*, these changes can be seen in the narrowed focus of the schizophrenia category, the elimination of psychodynamic etiological formulations, and the greater specificity of acute or reversible organic diagnoses. Psychoanalytic concepts, although still accepted by many, have returned to the periphery of psychiatry after having occupied a central position for many years.

The orientation of the *DSM*s from *DSM-III* on has been ostensibly behavioral. True behaviorists, however, still point to much implicit theorizing and vagueness in the supposedly operational terms. Taylor (1983), for example, was critical of the bias toward the medical model, the inclusion of many conditions he did not believe legitimately belong in a psychiatric diagnostic system, and axes II, III, and IV, which have not been adequately validated. He was referring to *DSM-III*, but the substance of criticisms such as these would apply as well to *DSM-III-R* and *DSM-IV*. Carson (1991) pointed out that, despite attempts to base the system empirically beginning with *DSM-III*, the underlying assumption has always been to perpetuate already established demarcations. According to him, empirical work has always begun with the implicit assumption that all that was required was fine-tuning. He suggested that "It does not in any obvious way admit of the possibility of breaking out of its own confines to emerge with a new and potentially more generative way of organizing the phenomena of mental disorder" (pp. 303–304). Most recently, McGorry et al. (1995) concluded that only modest agreement could be found among four different procedures used for assigning *DSM-III-R* psychotic disorders. The authors point out that this affects research studies as well as clinical practice. They indicate that, especially with first-episode psychosis:

> [M]isclassification can lead to iatrogenic effects because of the prognosis-based diagnostic categories with which we continue to work in psychosis. If even rigorous operational procedures in a research context can cross-sectionally misclassify people into a diagnostic group with an inherently pessimistic set of expectations linked to it, e.g., schizophrenia, this should be of concern to clinicians. (p. 223)

In other words, they questioned the validity of diagnoses being made daily with this system.

Also, as yet minimally incorporated into the *DSM*s is the growing professional interest in trauma and its aftermath. Two streams feed into this interest. Feminists in particular have incorporated it thoroughly into their worldview. But also interested in trauma is the group that forced the opening wedge into the diagnostic formulations that we do have: those studying and treating military veterans, primarily those from the Vietnam era. Feminists and allies in the mental health field have tried, so far unsuccessfully, to influence the *DSM* process into recognizing what they consider to be the major role trauma plays in a variety of emotional and mental disturbances. PTSD came into existence with *DSM-III*. *DSM-IV* has added acute stress disorder but did not recognize complex PTSD (Herman, 1992a) or any other equivalent.

Maria Root (1992) pointed out some of the difficulties in recognizing the impact and prevalence of trauma:

> (1) As time elapses since the original trauma, it becomes more difficult to connect symptoms to the initial event. And in fact, through a complex learning process, the symptomatology that is sequelae to traumatic experiences is indeed less directly related. (2) Over time the wounds of trauma are disguised by crises that require immediate attention. (3) Health care professionals are seldom trained in the area of victimization and trauma. (4) Researchers have approached the determination of trauma as though there are a limited number of "spaces" for what constitutes valid trauma. . . . (5) Our conceptual limitations may origi-

nate in a long-standing refusal to believe that atrocities initiated by other people indeed occur and do so with alarming frequency. (pp. 231–232)

Besides Root's differentiation of trauma into several global types—direct, insidious, and indirect, which can occur separately or in combination—she has also differentiated trauma in ways that impact the meanings attached to the experience. She distinguishes between trauma perceived to be either intended (malicious) or accidental and whether the experience occurs in isolation or with other (companion) victims (see Figure 3.1).

FIGURE 3.1
Categorization of Traumatic Events

Intent

Context		Malicious	Accidental
Isolation		Rape Child sexual abuse Child physical abuse Battering Vietnam experience Racial discrimination	Car accident Avalanche Hunting accident Burglary Miscarriage
Companion		Hostage experience Concentration camp Experience of war Dislocation	Fire Flood Earthquake Death of a child Train derailment Nuclear disaster

Source: Root (1992, p. 243).

Root emphasizes that the results of trauma differ with the difference in meaning attaching to it. Especially when it occurs with companion victims, it is easier to normalize both the psychological and physiological aftereffects.

Within the study of trauma, some new data stand the age-old differentiation between mind and body on its ear. A growing body of literature indicates that trauma, whether initially experienced physically or psychologically, has effects that cause possibly permanent changes in the central nervous system. As van der Kolk (1988) pointed out, this is a return to the ideas of Abraham Kardiner (1941), who first described the results of trauma as a "physioneurosis," that is, a mental disorder that affects both the mind and the body. In general, effects of mind on body or body on mind have been accepted, but permanent changes in the central nervous system from psychological events have not.

The only major theoretical material that has incorporated a feminist viewpoint at all is the newly expanding explication of trauma. Root (1992), however, indicates that trauma occurs in areas of personal, ethnic, and other cultural experiences in addition to those limited areas the traditional formalized system has (so far) reluctantly accepted. An important new study (Landrine, Klonoff, Gibbs, Manning, & Lund, 1995) has indicated that sexist discrimination accounts for additional variance in women's symptoms beyond that attributable to generic stressors. These findings give us a still more sophisticated view of the role of trauma. They suggest:

> [O]ne possible model is that generic life events, hassles, role-related gender-specific stressors (role overload, strain or conflict), and Lifetime Sexist Events operate as distal predictors of symptoms among women. Distal predictors are background or contextual variables that function as a diathesis, and are necessary but not sufficient to predict and explain symptoms. Thus, while the presence of the distal predictors may be said to characterize most if not all women's lives, most women do not exhibit significant psychiatric symptoms. . . . Recent (past year) sexist events and brutal/physical sexist discrimination (rape, battering) may operate as proximal predictors of symptoms among women, where a proximal predictor is a variable that is current or recent, is salient, and has a direct effect on symptoms. In the absence of a proximal predictor, distal variables alone produce mild symptoms. . . . [M]any women experience the distal predictors and these constitute a background level of chronic, high stress that places them at risk for symptoms. Yet, many women adapt to these distal conditions (via mediators such as coping skills and strong social support networks) and do not exhibit severe symptoms (but may exhibit mild ones) because of the absence of proximal predictors. (p. 487)

In support of Root, Klonoff and Landrine (1995) found that "women of color experience more frequent sexist discrimination than do White women in certain arenas" (p. 467).

The importance of the study of trauma has grown progressively in the past 25 years, but as we have seen, it only marginally touches the official classifications. We are only beginning to explicate all areas to which our newly emerging theory can apply and to more effectively differentiate among the effects of different kinds of trauma in different populations of women.

It is possible that behavior theory and/or an operational approach could incorporate this new range of concepts and ideas, but this as yet is only a potential, not a reality. Variables that are not recognized cannot become part of the system. In my view, however, operationalism is not inherently in opposition to the broader view feminists are insisting upon. The problem here is rather that the people who use this type of system still do not view the territory through a wide enough lens.

LACK OF CONCEPTUAL BASIS

A task force formed by the American Psychological Association to assess the need for an alternative diagnostic system concluded in its final report in 1977 that the diagnostic approach of *DSM-III*, then in preparation, was unsatisfactory for a number of reasons: Its disease-based model was inappropriately applied to problems in living; the specific categories were consistently unreliable; groupings were variously based on symptom clusters, antisocial behaviors, theoretical considerations, and developmental influences; categories were either created or deleted based on committee votes rather than on science; the labels had assumed strong judgmental qualities that frequently led to bias; and it offered little in the way of treatment indications or prediction of clinical outcome (Task Force, 1977). Most of these criticisms are still appropriate, although the manual has moved on to become *DSM-III-R* and now *DSM-IV*.

In an article offering his prediction of where psychology was headed, Raymond Cattell (1983) said of *DSM-III* that it is

> still Aristotelian in conception and not showing awareness of a Galilean transition to representation by degrees of individual trait dimensions interacting in lawful mechanisms.
>
> The categories are not even objectively statistically discovered, but are apparently the work of a committee. (p. 771)

Taylor (1983) approved the use of operational criteria for diagnoses used in *DSM-III* but pointed out that many had not been used before and that some seemed arbitrary and pseudospecific. In speaking of two particular diagnoses, for example, he commented: "An agoraphobic can't travel over five miles away from home by any means, or a depressed person must lose more than two pounds. Why five miles rather than one? Or two pounds and not six?" (p. 9). He recognized the operational intent of the new system but also that it was not as well based in research findings as its formulators would like us to believe. No data-based rationales for the particular cutoff points used can be demonstrated.

An even more stinging critique comes from within the psychiatric camp itself. Faust and Miner (1986) decried the very attempt to achieve objectivity in *DSM-III*, pointing out that this ought to be the goal in the first place and that the appearance of such objectivity in *DSM-III* is illusory: "Theory and inference have perhaps been reduced somewhat but eliminated nowhere—the document is replete with presuppositions and theoretical assumptions" (p. 963). Among the specific examples they offered was in the very definition of mental disorder. They pointed out that the essence of its definition is usually distress and impairment and that these criteria must be based on what they consider to be higher-level theoretical assumptions. In accord with what I have attempted to present they added that these criteria are "permeated by dominant social values and are shaped, in part, by the preference for a statistical definition of normality and abnormality" (p. 963). Faust and Miner also questioned the assumption of hierarchy rather than multidimensional ratings and suggested that this choice is not formed on any scientific criterion. They added that, despite the claim of atheoreticality, each disorder contained subtle assumptions about etiology. They found such assumptions in such aspects as the age specified for onset or the description of the disorder itself, items that had no basis in specific data. They pointed out, too, that the usual order in science is a progression from theory to fact rather than the reverse, as is presupposed in *DSM-III*. They also decried the overemphasis on reliability they detected in *DSM-III*, pointing out that reliability is one step on the road to validity but not a goal in itself, asserting that "in the long run, there is little to be gained by attempting to measure poorly understood things precisely and then multiplying our observations of them" (p. 966).

Although *DSM-III* was purportedly designed to offer more consistency and reliability in the process of diagnosis, many authors have pointed out that many problems in that regard still exist. Helzer and Coryell (1983) mentioned that, despite specified criteria for each diagnosis, one would need to know whether particular diagnosticians were using them "as a strict guide, a loose guide, or whether familiarity with the criteria is simply being used to shape the clinician's diagnostic concepts" (p. 1201). They also pointed out that each clinician tends to have his [sic] personal threshold for assessing symptomatology. For example, one clinician might consider a given report of sleep difficulty clinically significant while another does not. They suggested that "these thresholds are obviously influenced by one's training, one's colleagues, and the range of severity of symptomatology that one typically sees in a given clinical setting" (p. 1201).

These objections can be extended to encompass other sources of variability that Helzer and Coryell do not mention, including gender, age, and personal experiences with the symptom at issue that would call into play issues from the assessor's upbringing.

Almost any clinician who is aware of these issues can probably think of similar incidents in which a diagnostician dealt with a patient from a narrow perspective. One simple example I have seen was in the assessment of alcohol problems. I saw one clinician ignore a college-age client's statement that he drank several six-packs of beer daily because the examiner himself had done exactly the same during his college days. In many examples, however, the assessor's assumptions are less clear-cut. We have already discussed how mental patients' physical complaints are often disregarded. Such assumptions ignore the possibility that physical tests might generate information about physical ailments whose symptoms sometimes can mimic psychiatric syndromes. We also see the assumption that particular symptoms (whether physical or mental) automatically accompany increasing age. I have also seen several young men who, in assessing older women in particular, have demonstrated harshness in their manner, leading me (and any other women professionals who became aware of such behavior) to wonder about the nature of the relationships these men had with their own mothers or mother surrogates.

LACK OF OPENNESS TO INPUT

In a discussion about the American Psychological Association's attempt to formulate an alternative to *DSM-III*, Smith and Kraft (1983) pointed out that *DSM-III* uses a "language that is not common to the entire mental health culture," relying instead on symbols and a vocabulary that express "the world view of one professional subculture." They suggested a co-ownership arrangement among the mental health disciplines even as they conclude from a survey of psychologists that, while they rejected both the *DSM-III* model and descriptive behavioral analysis, there was little agreement on what might replace *DSM-III*.

The list of individuals who contributed to *DSM-IV* is quite long and impressive. Most have M.D.'s, but a respectable minority have Ph.D.'s. None, however, are identified with initials indicating social work, nursing, or other degrees. Even the extent to which Ph.D. psychologists seem to have been included is misleading, however. Although official liaisons from the American Psychological Association were appointed with great fanfare, they were never consulted during the process of writing *DSM-IV*. Smith and Kraft's suggestion about co-ownership has not become fact.

UNEXAMINED ASSUMPTIONS

Before *DSM-III* was published, an anthropologist did an interesting study whose published report never garnered much attention. He asked his students to write their own biographies in the form of psychiatric dossiers and to focus primarily on experiences they had that

> they would at the moment consider irrational, unintelligible, alien, or simply overreactions to environmental stress; experiences that, from a psychiatric standpoint, would be considered symptomatic of personality disorders, neurosis, or psychosis. (Movahedi, 1975, p. 193)

These were submitted anonymously and then evaluated independently by three judges (a psychologist, a graduate student in psychology, and Dr. Movahedi). Over 90% of the biographies were judged to fall into one of the three general categories of psychiatric disturbances. The author's point was that someone designated as a patient would be likely to negatively color the events he or she reported. Movahedi suggested that "the question of the methodological meaningfulness of psychiatric dossiers as a form of evidence in scientific reasoning should be given serious consideration" (p. 192). To the best of my knowledge, no one has followed through or discussed the implications of this interesting research finding. It accords with the findings of psychologist David Rosenhan, whose 1973 article in *Science* is still being referred to. In this article, he reported the results of a study in which eight pseudo-patients (actually students) were admitted to mental hospitals, having reported auditory hallucination symptoms of brief duration. The group was instructed to give up reporting symptoms after being admitted. The admitting diagnosis in all cases except one was schizophrenia, and on discharge, all were given the label of schizophrenia in remission. Although fellow patients often recognized the pseudopatients' "sanity" during their stay, there was no indication in the hospital records that any staff person ever questioned or doubted the presence of supposed illness in any of the cases.

In a later discussion (Rosenhan, 1975), he indicated that one of his major concerns was the effect of context on diagnosis and proposed several general remedies for the problems his study had exposed. Suggesting that the problem was not classification but poor and *mis*classification, he recommended strong evidence of validity before a classification is used. Spitzer (1976) strongly took issue with this recommendation, citing the need to make psychiatric diagnoses and similar decisions on the spot with less than perfect systems. Spitzer asserted that, had he been the diagnosing psychiatrist, he would have recognized the pseudopatients—an assertion that is hard to accept as anything more than the expression of his own ego.

The argument points up the pigeonholing problem that has plagued psychiatry's none too glorious history. Despite Spitzer's assurances that different psychiatric diagnoses result in different treatment (mainly different medication regimes in the present day) (Spitzer, 1976), individuality is certainly lost in inpatient settings, and it is easy to ignore individual circumstances there as well as outside the hospital, especially for the more serious ailments (Sarbin, 1990).

Incidentally, Movahedi's study, performed before *DSM-III* and the advent of axis II diagnoses, found that a higher percentage of females than males were labeled neurotic while males' dossiers were rated as personality disorders. The author interpreted these results, I think appropriately, as indicating that the female role was more likely than the male one to be considered neurotic. One need only think of the well-known Broverman study (1970) for confirmation. Movahedi moreover suggested that the male role was inextricably tied to the disorder formerly known as sociopathic personality. (See Kaplan [1983a] for confirmation of this point.)

It would be interesting to know how these results might look using the present system in which many symptoms, formerly labeled neurotic, are included as symptom patterns for many of the personality disorders on axis II that are diagnosed more often for women than men.

The Multiaxial Model

Axis II, designed for long-term or what could be considered characterological rather than symptomatic diagnosis, is the major contribution to a multiaxial mode of diagnosis in the American system. It was introduced in *DSM-III* and continues in *DSM-IV*. It is supposed to delineate long-term, stable aspects of psychological functioning. No actual discussion of the difference between diagnosing on axis I and axis II ever appeared in any one of the relevant *DSM*s. In adults, the personality disorders are diagnosed on axis II rather than axis I. For children and adolescents, developmental disorders were initially to be listed on axis II in *DSM-III*. In *DSM-III-R*, the mental retardation diagnoses were added to that axis. In *DSM-IV*, only the mental retardation diagnoses are listed under axis II. No reasons for these changes are given in the text of *DSM-IV*.

Livesley, Schroeder, Jackson, and Jang (1994) concluded that the separation of axis I and axis II diagnoses cannot be justified on the basis of either etiological considerations or temporal stability of symptoms or patterns. They suggest that there are pragmatic advantages for either separating these diagnoses or combining them on a single axis.

It is probably true that the existence of axis II has stimulated greater interest in the personality disorders in the literature. It is also true, however, that no adequate degree of reliability of the axis II diagnoses has been achieved (Mellsop, Varghese, Joshua, & Hicks, 1982; Moldin, Rice, Erlenmeyer-Kimling, & Squires-Wheeler, 1994). The criteria are vaguely and nonspecifically written and many apply to more than one disorder.

Erik Essen-Moller first proposed a multiaxial classification for the official Swedish classification of mental disorders as early as 1947. The two axes he proposed were symptom or syndrome, and etiology (Mezzich, 1979). Ottosson and Perris (1973) later elaborated on Essen-Moller's work, proposing as axes symptomatology, etiology, time frame, intensity, and certainty. As of 1985, a total of 15 multiaxial systems had been proposed, each differing in the

number of axes used, although usually they included phenomenology, etiology, time, and adaptive functioning (Stieglitz, Fahndrich, & Helmchen, 1988).

The work on multiaxial aspects that began with *DSM-III* seems
to have occurred independently of this and related work. Many
critics of the *DSM*s have pointed out that they do not truly represent a multiaxial model since they do not deal with different
dimensions in arriving at a diagnosis. The critics indicate that the
DSM is actually quite traditional in its concept of diagnosis, with
standard diagnoses being made on axis I and to some degree also
on axis II. It has turned out that in actual practice diagnoses on axes
III, IV, and V are rarely made and, even then, rarely considered. In
no way does diagnosis on these axes affect the primary diagnosis
on either axis I or axis II. The goal of a truly multiaxial system is a
mutually independent record of data about various aspects of the
patient on each axis (Stieglitz, Fahndrich, & Helmchen, 1988). This
the *DSM*s do not do (Cooper, 1988).

The Medical Model

One unacknowledged aspect of the medical model that has been
applied in the *DSM*s is that of a hierarchy of diagnosis. For a long
time, it was assumed in medicine that one diagnosis should be
assigned per patient and that the treatment of the one underlying
disorder would, most directly and effectively, treat and alleviate
all of the patient's symptoms. While the growth of geriatric medicine has focused treatment on chronic diseases and raised the
awareness in medicine that a patient may have more than one disease, the diagnostic hierarchy implicit in the *DSM*s has not been
examined. In accord with the tradition that begins with Kraepelin,
the general assumption is that there is a hierarchy of psychiatric
ailments that goes in the following order: organic disorders, schizophrenia, manic-depressive or bipolar illness, and neurotic illnesses. The hierarchy is important since it implies that any disorder could cause symptoms of disorders lower in the hierarchy.
Such research as has been done suggests that anyone having any
psychiatric disorder is more likely to also have any other psychiatric disorder, wherever it may be in the standard hierarchy (Boyd
et al., 1984).

The introductory sections of *DSM-III* and *DSM-III-R* discuss
hierarchy of diagnoses, but the comparable section of *DSM-IV* does
not. In addition, *DSM-IV* seems to have toned down indications in

the discussion of one diagnosis that it is not to be used in the presence of another. There does not seem to have been any discussion of this apparent change in philosophy. It should therefore be interesting to observe whether or not diagnosticians are aware of the change—or will become aware of it—and how the change will affect the actual process of diagnosis.

Although *DSM-IV* often does not include a formal attribution of etiology for many of the diagnoses it now lists, the inclusion of labels in a manual published by the American Psychiatric Association strongly implies a physical (medical) basis for these diagnostic categories. That is one reason many have objected to the inclusion in the manual of what Szasz called "problems in living" even when they are not formally called psychiatric disorders (Szasz, 1961). This especially applies to smoking, gambling, and grieving, among others, which are listed in *DSM-IV*.

The use of terms like "disorder" and the explicit use of category names also strongly implies that a diagnosis listed in a *DSM* represents an actual entity theoretically comparable to a medical diagnosis such as pneumonia or diabetes. The movement in the field toward dimensional (as opposed to categorical) diagnosis has the potential to alleviate this problem and, incidentally, move the system toward a more truly multiaxial form. Some examples of alternative systems will be discussed later.

Roger Blashfield (1984), a psychologist, has suggested that the term *medical model* is emotionally loaded. He strongly stated that it has become associated with issues of professional jurisdiction during a time when the proportion of psychiatrists among mental health workers in general has been declining and other professions such as psychology have become recognized by insurance companies and other providers. This concern, in his view, has been interwoven with the question of what type of theory would in the long run best explain psychopathology.

Feminist complaints about the perpetuation of the medical model revolve around power issues that are almost always felt whenever physicians in general and female patients interact (Tavris, 1992).

Ignoring Political Implications

One other relatively unexamined assumption in our official diagnostic system is that what is always being described is an inner condition of an individual. This is true even though the *DSM* manuals do note on occasion that the deviancy that is labeled as a mental disorder shows up in conflicts between an individual and society. They nevertheless focus on this inner state in their definitions. Ignored, of course, is the fact that in the past society has viewed such activities as homosexual behavior and masturbation as pathological, but does not now. This perspective cannot adequately account for the ways in which changes in social views cause changes in what is called psychopathology without any appreciable change in the inner states of persons previously labeled.

Blashfield and Livesley (1991) recently summarized the problem very succinctly:

> Because psychiatric classification serves as a nomenclature, a psychiatric classification is necessarily political. The terms in a classification form the nouns for the language of the field. As a result, struggles over who controls the language are basic to the dominance issues among different theoretical and professional groups. The DSM-III sought to defuse some of these issues by developing a putatively atheoretical stance in regard to etiology in order to increase general acceptance of the classification. Although the intent is understandable, the effect of being generally atheoretical was to drive the political issues underground. As a result, some of the assumptions underlying the DSM-III and DSM-III-R classifications are implicit. This makes it difficult to test important issues about these classificatory systems. By attempting to avoid the inherent political issues of a classification, a paradoxical effect has been to bring the political versus scientific tension over classification into greater focus, although any dialogue has been suppressed. Part of the process inherent to scientific advances is the dialogue and competition between different theoretical schools of thought. By attempting to avoid the politics of classification, the recent DSMs may have unintentionally retarded scientific growth by blunting that dialogue. (p. 268)

In other words, under the assumptions of the recent *DSMs* (the article was written before *DSM-IV* was completed, but the statement applies to it equally as well as it did to *DSM-III* and *DSM-III-R*), there seems to be little way to advance the process of classification except through exposing its political nature and, by extrapolation, suggesting alternative paradigms. These will be discussed in more detail later.

CHAPTER 4

Why Diagnose?

KROLL (1979) WROTE THAT the third edition of the *Diagnostic and Statistical Manual of Mental Disorders*, published in 1980, represented the most specific and detailed classification system of mental disorders in use in the world. As its successor, that designation now belongs to *DSM-IV* (1994). It is the present official nomenclature of American psychiatry, the result of a process that has moved back and forth over some 40 years between somewhat different assumptions about the etiology of mental disorders. Those assumptions and how they have changed have been discussed. This chapter explores the assumptions underlying the process of categorization and systematization itself.

Kety (1975) suggested that the four requirements of a classification system useful for research in biology could be applied to mental disorders. First, there has to be order and differentiation in the matters being examined, including human behavior. Second, commenting on the phenomenological basis of biological classification systems, he indicated that we nevertheless need to maintain standards by which to differentiate valid phenomena and primary data from inferences and hypotheses. Third, he suggested that a useful classification system "does not beg important questions ... which it is the very purpose of the classification to help solve" (p. 12). As a failure to observe this rule, for instance, Kety cited the difficulty in distinguishing between what usually is called endogenous depression ("based primarily on special heredito-constitutional factors, thus originating predominantly *within* the organism itself and affecting the nervous system *directly*" [Campbell, 1989]) and reactive depression ("secondary to, resulting from or precipitated by an identifiable happening" [Campbell, 1989]). He pointed out that too many layers of assumptions that move too far away from

101

the phenomenal experience of patients have to be made in this distinction, as in many others, because obvious symptoms themselves do not suggest any specific etiology. Speculations about etiology, he felt, are inappropriate in a classification system unless and until they are verified by accepted rules of scientific evidence—something hard to achieve in this field. Fourth, any system must be able to recognize and entertain uncertainty—a requirement that speaks to difficulties in the thought processes and emotions of mental health workers.

Strictly speaking, Kety spoke to the requirements of a classification system and not its purpose, although he implies that research is an important underlying purpose for classification in mental health just as it is in biology. This perspective on diagnosis, however, is too narrow because each system, including our own changing system, reflects the values and assumptions of the society that uses it. Until recently, almost all psychiatrists in the United States, particularly those with organizational power, have been male and white. With the power of the male medical establishment behind them, any system devised by this group will clearly reflect primarily white male values and attitudes about such matters as the role of women, ethnicity, and homosexuality, in addition to current professional values about etiology in general. No claim of objectivity for any diagnostic classification in mental health can be substantiated. That being so, let us look at the purpose of making diagnoses in the first place. Is it, as Kety implies, purely or mostly research?

In the same report in which Kety's paper appeared, Nunnally (1975) suggested three purposes for classifying people. One is to take account of salient attributes about them. A second is to provide mental health workers with a sense of comfort about aspects of human behavior that are not well understood nor easily treated—a purpose that has rarely been acknowledged in the field, although, as we have seen, it was implied by Kety. Third, it facilitates communication among mental health workers.

For the sake of completeness, let us mention here that Robert Spitzer, a primary architect of *DSM-III* and *DSM-III-R,* has also indicated his view of the purposes of diagnosis. Although he has been a strong advocate for research as a basis for diagnosis, he clearly stated his views in purely clinical terms:

It enables mental health professionals to *communicate* with each other about the subject matter of their concern, *comprehend* the pathological processes involved in psychiatric illness, and *control* psychiatric disorders. Control consists of the ability to predict out-come, prevent the disorder from developing, and treat it once it has developed [emphasis in original]. (1976, p. 465)

For Spitzer, then, communication is a primary purpose, but he also emphasized understanding, prevention, and treatment as impor-tant other purposes.

Blashfield and Draguns (1976b), beginning as Kety did with the zoological literature on taxonomy and applying it to psychiatry, identified five general purposes for classification. It provides: (1) a basis for communication within the field, (2) a basis for the retrieval of information from the literature, (3) a descriptive system in order to facilitate study, (4) a basis for scientific prediction, and (5) a source of concepts for the development of theory. They did not mention professionals' need to have labels to increase their own comfort level, nor do they mention prevention or treatment directly.

None of the purposes suggested by Blashfield and Draguns spoke either to any underlying value orientation (rather than a the-oretical orientation) that might unite a diagnostic system or to any external practical circumstances that might influence or even per-petuate it—both clearly issues in the nebulous realm of mental ill-ness that will be discussed later along with the question of how diagnostic systems are actually used. But first, since Blashfield and Draguns have taken a more comprehensive approach to the subject than others have, we will discuss their ideas in detail.

BLASHFIELD AND DRAGUNS'S STATED PURPOSES

Communication

Blashfield and Draguns (1976b, p. 575) quoted from the intro-duction of *DSM-II*, current at the time of their article:

In selecting suitable diagnostic terms for each rubric, the Com-mittee has chosen terms which it thought would facilitate maxi-mum communication with the profession and reduce confusion and ambiguity to a minimum (American Psychiatric Association, 1968, p. viii)

Blashfield and Draguns pointed out that those who use a system in clinical diagnostic practice will incorporate any alternate system only if they accept its terms. They suggest, following Deutsch (1966), that a new classification is most likely to evolve as an initially informal jargon within a small group of scientists. As the political power and social influence of this group increases, its terminology experiences wider and more general acceptance. (p. 575)

They further commented that the process by which this occurs is itself "a phenomenon worthy of systematic empirical investigation by social psychologists and sociologists" (p. 575). Thus, they explicitly acknowledged that the process of classification is not scientific but instead political and social. In broad terms, then, one may say that what is taught to and therefore known by individual professionals (categories, but this point has broader implications) determines for the most part what other professionals will know in the future. Meanwhile, new ideas and new information have a hard time becoming known enough to be taught.

Information Retrieval

Blashfield and Draguns (1976b) quote from Sneath and Sokol, eminent botanical taxonomists who wrote, "A plant's name is a key to its literature" (p. 575). Particularly as literature accumulates, a change in any classification or coding system is likely to make it harder for researchers to find existing information, although it might also provide access to previously neglected sources and differing slants on existing information.

This fact of professional life is becoming even more significant in the era of automated information retrieval. A computer program can only do what it is told. It can only retrieve information coded by particular key words determined by humans. If humans have not noted relationships between or among key words, potentially relevant information that might be in the literature cannot make its way into professional lore. Again, what is taught determines what is known because that has influenced how categories are formulated and coded in databases and what can readily be retrieved for future use. New information has a harder time becoming known, especially if it requires new categories or key words.

Description

Ideally, according to Blashfield and Draguns,

One of the purposes of a classificatory system is to provide a basis for describing important similarities and differences between psychiatric patients. If the diagnostic groupings are homogeneous, a patient's diagnosis should furnish a reasonably accurate summary of the important characteristics of the patient. (p. 576)

They add, however, that "an adequate classification of psychopathology need not necessarily be so structured that patients with the same diagnosis have identical symptoms (i.e., that they constitute a monothetic classification)" (p. 576). They point out that only a high correlation between a particular symptom and membership in a diagnostic class is required. Generalizations are made on the basis of similarities; individual differences are not considered and drop out of sight. Once again, what is taught becomes what is known, and facts that are not used by the system drop out of sight and are not considered further.

Prediction

In effect, prediction, along with description, comprises Blashfield and Draguns's clinical usefulness criteria. They suggest that classification "can override the potentially damaging effects of labelling if it provides clear indications for the type of therapy to be used and for the formulation of prognostic statements" (p. 577). They suggest also that their stated purposes for diagnosis overlap and in particular, that the predictive value of a classification can be related to its clinical acceptability. Arguing against opponents of labeling, they indicate that "the social justification of psychiatric classification can hinge on the demonstration of its predictive value," that is, whether or not it can result in appropriate, effective treatment.

While gains have been made in relating diagnosis to potential therapy and/or outcome, in the mental health field this process is still in its infancy. Theoretically, of course, the disorders of individuals with some particular diagnoses may generally be assumed to move along some hypothesized course. Also, since mental health professionals are human beings subject to the same kind of psychological processes as others, the role of an observer's expectations in what is perceived becomes a factor here as it does in other circumstances. Although it has not been directly applied to the mental health arena, research in experimenter and observer bias has clearly demonstrated in general that no such thing as a detached observer exists (Farber, 1990). What is more, at the psychological level we know that people live up or down to the expectations of the authorities who have power over them.

Theory Formation

The implication here is that psychiatric classification can be used as a basis for formulating a theory of psychopathology.

> The characteristics of a classification then set the limits for the type of theory which can evolve from it. Conversely, a theory determines the characteristics of a classification evolved within its framework. The choice of classificatory concepts guides the conduct of research and organizes explanatory principles. (Blashfield & Draguns, 1976b, p. 578)

This idea sounds fine, but it is not, however, how diagnostic systems actually operate in real life. Instead, changes in the level of professional acceptability of existing theoretical positions have changed the classification system, not vice versa. Diagnostic concepts rarely result in new or different or more elaborate explanatory principles.

Kety, Nunnally, and Blashfield and Draguns all agree that classification facilitates communication and research. Kety and Nunnally did not comment on its use for theory formation, one of Blashfield and Draguns's stated purposes that actual events do not seem to justify.

PURPOSES IN ACTUAL USE

Before looking at the present American system, *DSM-IV*, in terms of how it fulfills Blashfield and Draguns's suggested purposes, three more possible purposes should be added. Each has practical implications, although in different ways. They exist on a very different plane than the purposes formulated by Blashfield and Draguns and others.

Clinical Usefulness

One is the actual extent to which a system is clinically useful to practitioners. Even those who profoundly object to formal diagnostic classification and labeling indulge in "diagnostic thinking." We have discussed how that occurs whenever a clinician decides something that the client or patient does or says fits into one or another of his or her private (often unarticulated) diagnostic categories, suggesting that one treatment is likely to be more fruitful than another. Ordinarily, this type of diagnosis is a continually evolving process. While formal diagnostic classifications may form the basis for some professionals' personal schema, they definitely do not form the basis for all.

Earlier discussion has touched on some of the implications of clinical usefulness. The American Psychiatric Association has attempted to address this issue by publishing case books and treatment manuals keyed directly to its diagnostic system (Spitzer, Gibbon, Skodol, Williams, & First, 1994). This endeavor might be more reasonable and justifiable if the system really had a fully (or even largely) agreed upon theoretical and/or scientific basis and if it incorporated some of the issues (the use of the medical model, for example) that professional and other groups feel are missing.

Perhaps the best example of where the clinical usefulness of *DSM-IV* can be disputed is in the use of axis II diagnoses, particularly that of the borderline personality disorder. As has been pointed out, research studies have documented that large numbers of psychiatric patients given various official diagnoses have experienced chronic physical, psychological, and sexual abuse during their upbringing. Many noted professionals have stated that it might well be feasible to consider the possibility that many individuals, particularly women, who have been diagnosed as having borderline personality disorders (Barnard & Hirsch, 1985; Gross et al., 1980; Herman & van der Kolk, 1987) or even multiple personality disorders (Coons & Milstein, 1984; Herman & van der Kolk, 1987, Putnam et al., 1986; Saltman & Solomon, 1982) can be better treated if they are thought of as suffering long-term chronic post-traumatic stress disorder (PTSD). The implications for treatment are quite different for PTSD than they are for the personality disorders. Despite pressure even from within, the American Psychiatric Association did not see fit to include a proposed disease of extreme stress or other similar entity in *DSM-IV*. Rather than expanding the role of trauma, it even saw fit to narrow the conceptualization of trauma encompassed by PTSD. Professionals who have focused on the effects of trauma have found it particularly difficult to accept the implications of the axis II diagnoses.

Another aspect of clinical usefulness pertains directly to how a diagnostic system is being used. In the strictest sense, it is not the fault of a system if it is used in ways other than those planned by those who devised it. How it is used, however, does represent important information that must be considered. Stuart Kirk and Herb Kutchins (1988) reported the results of a survey of how social workers use *DSM-III*. They found that their respondents reported

knowledge of what could only be considered intentional misuse of
DSM-III. This took the form of both under- and overdiagnosis,
depending on the circumstances. As a practicing clinician, I am
well aware of the phenomenon that Kirk and Kutchins reported
and the rationales clinicians use when they do this, but the literature rarely mentions, much less discusses, these practices, which
continue to this day. They do not change as the *DSM* is revised
because the underlying influences on clinicians have not changed
appreciably (Brown, 1990).

As Kirk and Kutchins reported and from my own clinical experiences, overdiagnosis is most likely to occur when reimbursement
is being provided by an insurance carrier or other third-party.
Third-party payers do not reimburse all the possible diagnoses that
can be made from the *DSM*s. Frequently, for example, they do not
pay when family, marital, and other interpersonal difficulties are
diagnosed with so-called V codes, which are not considered to represent official psychiatric disorders. One way around this problem
is to diagnose these and other less severe problems as anxiety or
depression. Often this is done with the collusion of clients, since
they also benefit when medical insurance pays a portion of their
bill for outpatient psychotherapy. There is no reason to assume that
this practice is likely to diminish when third-party payers increasingly regulate the practices of mental health workers.

Underdiagnosis means that a clinician chooses a less severe diagnosis than is indicated. Kirk and Kutchins (1988) refer to this as
"the least noxious diagnosis" or "mercy diagnosis" (p. 229). It is
less likely to be done in collusion with the client, although it may.
It is most often done to spare the client's feelings, to minimize negative information to an insurance company, and to avoid the stigmatizing social effects of the more severe diagnoses. It probably
happens more often when the client or patient has celebrity status
or is related in some way to another worker in the same facility or
to a clinician's personal friend. It can also result from some form of
identification with the patient. Perhaps she or he is a struggling
college student or the son or daughter of professionals. The mercy
aspect of the diagnosis eliminates some of the label's excess baggage that would have to be carried by a patient who later comes
under public scrutiny in the outside world.

Yet another relevant issue remains. Individual clinicians may not
use the diagnostic manual as fully or comprehensively as it was
designed to be used. Practitioners may feel that they know what
symptoms or signs indicate particular diagnoses and therefore

may not pay enough attention to the manual's indications of how many signs need to be present. In practice, any individual clinician's reliability is practically never checked either with other practitioners or with the requirements stated in the manual for a particular diagnosis. Jampala, Sierles, and Taylor (1988) reported one of the few attempts to study the real-world circumstances under which diagnosis is done. They surveyed graduating psychiatric residents (who would ordinarily be most expected to have studied the manual recently) for the signs and symptoms they required to diagnose major depression, mania, or schizophrenia. They found that none used all the inclusion and exclusion criteria listed in *DSM-III*, current at the time of the study. There is no reason to expect that mental health workers would use later editions of the *DSMs* any less casually.

Add to this psychiatrists' tendency to label as sick persons who are not, in the belief that assigning a diagnosis will cause less harm than not. Much in the literature demonstrates the shocking wrongness of this viewpoint, particularly when the effects of institutionalization, drug side effects, social class, gender, and race are considered (Brown, 1987).

All the problems of clinical usefulness potentially undermine, although indirectly, the usefulness of the diagnostic system as a research tool. If a category is used incorrectly for whatever reason, any research information collected and any subsequent correlation made about prognosis or preferred treatment based on it, for example, is suspect. Such practices represent sources of variance that are not ordinarily controlled for or otherwise taken into account. Most often it is just assumed that such factors do not exist, an attitude that severely compromises research in the entire area of mental illness.

It has also been demonstrated that most clinicians, quite apart from the issues being discussed here, consider the *DSM* to be more useful administratively than clinically (Robins & Helzer, 1986). Many would cease using it if they were not compelled to do so (Brown, 1990). The fact that labeling does not help much in treatment planning is clear, while most clinicians recognize that it aids communication within an agency and especially with outside groups (insurance companies, for example).

Light (1980) demonstrated that psychiatric residents, in response to conflicting role expectations, informally used four different diagnostic frameworks simultaneously. They used the formal *DSM* categories because they were required to but also because it satisfied organizational and legal requirements and permitted easy communication within the hospital or agency, the state mental health system, and the profession. They also used what Light called "managerial diagnoses" for the task of daily management. These included categories like "acting up," "suicidal," and others. On the other hand, they used what Light called "therapeutic diagnoses" in discussing the process of their patients in therapy. Lastly, Light found "dynamic diagnoses," which the psychiatric residents themselves considered to be the most valid. These were based on psychoanalytic conceptualizations of the patients in terms of areas of life like work, love, anger, and loss. Phil Brown (1987) suggests that psychoanalytic terminology may now be less prevalent and suggested adding a framework of "drug-related diagnoses." In this framework, patients would be diagnosed in terms of their past, present, and future response to medication, and their response would be used to support a specific *DSM* diagnosis, whether this information is contained within a *DSM* or not.

Communication with Third Parties

The other proposed addition to the criteria that I would like to suggest is about external but nevertheless important matters that have already been alluded to. Perhaps they could be considered a broad extension of Blashfield and Draguns's first stated purpose, that of communication in the field. Because of its practical significance, it is worth discussing separately. I am speaking of communication to external agents and agencies that surround the field of mental health and determine how mental health services are financially supported and to whom they are given—specifically, communication with insurance companies and government entities such as Medicare.

This is extremely important because, since the publication of *DSM-III* in 1980, the American Psychiatric Association system has been adopted, even swallowed in toto, by all the external funding agencies in the United States. If a diagnosis is not in *DSM-IV*, it is not now considered relevant and is not funded. The kind of recognition of what has by default become the official American system also holds for the nation's criminal and civil justice systems. In questioning this activity, I will ask later if *DSM-IV* is the very best mode of communication that we can use and what the results of this use are.

The dispute between the establishment and feminist practitioners, for example, spills over into the area of communication with funding agencies and other entities. If a battered woman's visible injuries are minor enough to suggest that she might not have feared for her life during the beating, it may no longer be possible to use a diagnosis of PTSD to get funding for her treatment or qualify her for support and possible redress within the legal system, despite the fact that she shows symptoms listed in the manual. (See chapter 3 for discussion of the change in criteria for using PTSD as a diagnosis.) Verbal abuse and sexual harassment on the job may also not qualify her for a diagnosis of PTSD even though her symptoms may fit the category very well. We raise here the question of how well the existing system corresponds with the moral and social values of the society in which it functions. Besides women, it also influences how minority groups are dealt with (Landrine, 1992).

The Comfort of Professionals

Among those who have formally addressed the issue of the purposes of classification, Nunnally (1975) was the only one who discussed the need to maintain and promote the comfort levels of mental health professionals. It is nevertheless true that having a label to assign does give comfort to the labeler, particularly when various assumptions about the person being labeled follow in a somewhat automatic fashion. Today, for example, to call someone schizophrenic implies a particular course of treatment (medication) and presumably continuing progression; that is, the patient will never fully recover. Perhaps the need for such a comfort level at least partly explains all the classification systems humans develop.

Scientists should be able to acknowledge that they are human and that some of their needs are served by what they do. Accepting this fact and making it public should ultimately further the cause of science. That would be better than perpetuating the fiction that it plays no part. Only when it is public can it be evaluated properly as part of the general mix. Neither psychiatrists, nor psychologists, nor social workers, nor nurses become gods when they achieve their professional status. To acknowledge that we have professional needs and investments in the systems we develop might just make us more humble. We need to recognize that human beings are more complex than any of our systems allow for.

EVALUATING CLASSIFICATION SYSTEMS

Besides commenting on the purposes of diagnosis, Blashfield and Draguns (1976a) also offered four criteria by which a psychiatric classification system could be judged: reliability, coverage, descriptive validity, and predictive validity. These criteria pertain primarily to the scientific or heuristic value of the classification scheme. The formulators of *DSM-III* and *DSM-IV* heavily emphasized reliability, which will be discussed in more detail later.

Robins and Helzer (1986) concluded that the breadth of coverage of *DSM-III* exists for administrative rather than clinical or research purposes—a view that easily applies as well to *DSM-IV*. That very breadth has exposed these manuals to criticism about the extent to which problems in living in addition to mental disorders have been brought under the umbrella of the medical model.

Validity is, however, a key point. It is clear that our present state of knowledge does not allow us to fully ascertain the validity of a diagnosis in terms of symptomatology, response to treatment, course of "illness," and possible etiological factors. Robins and Helzer (1986) suggested that possible answers lie with the results of epidemiological studies. The possibility of predicting the course of an ailment also relates to establishing the validity of a diagnosis. Note, however, that some of the problems already mentioned are possible unacknowledged sources of error in such studies.

Mezzich (1979) identified three different types of validity for evaluating diagnostic systems: descriptive, consensual, and predictive. He referred to descriptive validity as the agreement with patient data, implying that homogeneity within diagnostic groups exist independently of the labeler. Consensual validity refers to the extent to which a given system is acceptable to experienced clinicians. Mezzich suggested that, in actuality, this type of validity underlies most established systems. Predictive validity indicates the ability of a system to predict clinically such things as the course of the disorder and treatment results.

It is possible to argue that our present system does not show significant predictive validity and only a limited degree of descriptive validity. All of this shows the imperfection of our present state of knowledge and suggests that the value of any diagnostic system must reside for now in the extent to which we can ascertain that it fulfills the requirements for general usefulness or, in Mezzich's terms, consensual validity.

Evaluating DSM-IV

How does *DSM-IV* fulfill or fail to fulfill the purposes stated by Blashfield and Draguns? For example, in order for a diagnostic system to aid in professional communication, there must be some degree of agreement about terminology and underlying etiology. In the United States, there has been continuing controversy on these points. One only has to look at the oscillation over the years in the terms used by the systems in use, and the disputes among theoretical viewpoints that are not based in empirical evidence.

Another problem in the area of communication is that all mental health professions have been asked to use a system devised exclusively by psychiatry. Organized psychology has been unhappy about this for many years, with the emphasis on the medical model coming in for the most criticism. Psychiatry, psychology, social work, and nursing each have different traditions and bring different emphases to bear when working with individuals who receive diagnoses. Yet, with the exception of only minor and almost cosmetic participation in the process leading to *DSM-IV* by a few psychologists, only psychiatry has had a hand in formulating the diagnostic systems that all the professions are now obliged by the marketplace to use for external communication.

Once we move beyond the framework of the established professions per se to the different value systems of feminists, gay rights activists, and those who focus on ethnic and racial diversity, communication breaks down even further because the underlying value systems of the groups are so much more divergent. We have already pointed out how the concerns of these diverse groups have clearly not been incorporated into the current official diagnostic standard or even acknowledged in the process.

This exclusion particularly affects information retrieval. The underlying value systems of feminists and gay rights activists cause our categories to be very different from those of the established diagnosticians. This difference, for the very first time, became public during the controversy that raged over disputed categories in *DSM-III-R*. Feminists said that psychological and physical trauma plays a significant part in the etiology of the proposed category of self-defeating personality, for example, and indicated that professionals who do not code and classify with that in mind will not be able to retrieve the appropriate information about these women, whether for treatment or for scientific study (Rosewater, 1985; Walker, 1985).

One who does not code adequately cannot study appropriately. This truth applies to the now eliminated diagnosis of ego-dystonic homosexuality (Malyon, 1986) as well as to the diagnostic categories that feminists fought in the 1980s. If the social circumstances that produce someone who is troubled about being homosexual are not considered, how valid is any study made about homosexuality? If a physical disorder like premenstrual syndrome, one only comparatively recently recognized as such, is dealt with as a psychiatric disorder without recognition of its biological underpinnings, how can it be appropriately studied? All of this, of course, also affects the process of prediction, the most immediately significant aspect of which is arriving at appropriate treatment.

Social trends have played a large part in the changes that have taken place in psychiatric diagnosis from its beginnings until now. Parallel to the professional trends alluded to earlier, changes in the social climate, some greater acceptance of sexuality in its variations, and changes in society's views of women (as well as continued persistence of older views in some circles) can also be traced in the history of diagnostic categories. It is difficult to argue that the particular changes and blind spots generated by broader social trends are related to any research data, whatever the rhetoric used.

It was not research that caused psychiatrists to vote to eliminate the homosexuality diagnostic category in 1973 (Bayer, 1981), nor to refuse until now to recognize the political implications of retaining a separate diagnosis for difficulties with homosexual feelings that other diagnostic categories (anxiety disorder, etc.) could easily encompass. It is not research that determined that stereotypes of the female role in society (histrionic personality, passive personality) be given psychiatric diagnoses while it takes caricatures of the male social role (antisocial personality) to rate a psychiatric diagnosis (Kaplan, 1983a; Kass, Spitzer, & Williams, 1983). To remedy this inequity, Paula Caplan and her associates have proposed delusional dominating personality disorder as a diagnosis for males that results from rigid masculine socialization and includes behavior harmful to oneself and others in one's sphere (Pantony & Caplan, 1991). It has not been incorporated in part because the still largely male establishment does not accept the behavior described as symptomatic.

It is unlikely, too, that research dictated the differences in the criteria for the diagnosis of the sexual dysfunction disorders of premature ejaculation and inhibited female orgasm in *DSM-III*. In the first instance, the man determined when the diagnosis should be made by his own judgment that his ejaculation occurred too soon. In the second instance, the clinician determined when the diagnosis was to be given to a woman. He (used advisedly) was the one who determined that sufficient stimulation has occurred so that the woman's failure to reach orgasm merited the diagnosis of inhibited female orgasm. No specification of who decides that there has been an adequate phase of sexual excitement is, however, in the criteria for the diagnosis of inhibited male orgasm (American Psychiatric Association, 1980). Doesn't this difference in the weight given to what men and women tell about themselves say volumes about psychiatric attitudes toward men and women? The blatantly sexist implications were cleaned up somewhat in *DSM-III-R* and were carefully made at least cosmetically nonsexist in *DSM-IV,* although they undoubtedly continue to exist in the minds of many diagnosticians.

UNEXAMINED VALUES AND IMPLICIT ASSUMPTIONS

Perhaps the most fundamental questions for a diagnostic system to answer are how well it and its categories correspond with the mores of the larger society and whether they should so correspond. I obviously think they should.

Feminists within the mental health professions have been progressively identifying the male power assumptions that underlie the official system. For examples, see Lerman (1986), Brown (1994), and Walker (1994). Also see Steinem (1994), who represents the larger feminist community outside the mental health arena. Others have been looking at the assumption that symptoms mean the same thing regardless of the ethnic and/or racial background of the person exhibiting them, and are bringing up the ethnic and racial stereotypes of the person who has the power to establish the diagnosis (Landrine, 1992).

Mezzich, Fabrega, and Kleinman (1992) pointed out that some of the underlying assumptions of the *DSMs,* especially the concept of a mind-body dichotomy and the lack of balance in considering biological and psychosocial factors, are strongly rooted in majority American culture and are severely limited in their applicability to the growing numbers of ethnic minorities in our population. They also indicated the *DSMs'* inadequacies in distinguishing between pathological and normative behaviors in ethnic populations and their difficulties in dealing with the wide variety of cultural idioms of distress. Eisenbruch (1992) suggested that the growing use of PTSD with refugee groups ignores differences in how distress is expressed, how disorders are classified, and how distress might be ameliorated. The finger here is thus pointed at unexamined assumptions embedded in the system itself.

We live in a society that is increasingly diverse along a vast array of dimensions. The official diagnostic nomenclature does not in any significant way take into account that there are many societies and subsocieties within our larger one and that the viewpoint of generally older, prosperous, established, white men in the United States whose intellectual tradition is Eurocentric is not wide enough to deal effectively with what exists outside their world-view. Some other approach is obviously required, although it does not yet seem to be available.

CHAPTER 5

Exploring Alternatives

DESPITE THE PROMINENCE of the psychiatric *DSMs*, they do not provide the only approach to classification. Hidden in the professional literature are descriptions of several other approaches that have been taken either by individuals in various health disciplines or by their professional organizations. This chapter discusses and evaluates some of the more fully developed alternative systems.

A NURSING SYSTEM

Some 10 years ago, I learned for the first time that the nursing profession had its own general diagnostic system that includes provision for nursing care of psychiatric patients. Speculating about why I had never heard about this system, I thought about how few members of the mental health establishment have considered the question of diagnosis in anything like a critical manner. Feminist mental health workers had not been dealing with the subject with any seriousness until the dispute arose about the controversial diagnoses proposed for *DSM-III-R*. Only since then has the subject been broadly discussed and studied.

Kritek (1985) provided a brief history of the nursing diagnostic system. The first conference to deal with the issue took place in 1973. By 1983, a separate association, the North American Nursing Diagnosis Association (NANDA), had been formed for those nurses and nursing scholars interested in "the systematic identification, investigation, classification, and utilization of nursing diagnoses" (Kritek, 1985, p. 3). The diagnostic system the nursing profession has developed deals with the entire range of nursing practice and not just its psychiatric aspects. The perspective it provides is quite different from the psychiatric diagnosis system.

In 1978, Carol Soares discussed the difference between medical diagnosis and nursing diagnosis. She suggested that a medical diagnosis dealt with the pathological state of the patient and also with the implied right of medicine to treat the diagnosed state. She saw nursing diagnosis, on the other hand, as defining altered patterns of human functioning or problems that could be dealt with by nurses independently but in accord with the medical diagnosis. The identification of problems requires analysis of the patient's unmet needs as well as potential nursing actions that could supply, support, and/or remove something to meet those needs (Soares, 1978).

As the NANDA categories developed, nine patterns of potential difficulty were identified: (1) exchanging, (2) communicating, (3) relating, (4) valuing, (5) choosing, (6) moving, (7) perceiving, (8) knowing, and (9) feeling. Many of the subdivisions under these patterns related to physical or potentially physical issues, especially those under exchanging and moving, although some of the moving categories can have psychological/psychiatric implications (such as activity intolerance, fatigue, sleep pattern disturbance, diversional activity deficit, feeding self-care deficit, bathing/hygiene self-care deficit, dressing/grooming self-care deficit, and relocation stress syndrome).

All the other patterns deal almost exclusively with at least potentially psychological and/or environmental or social issues. The only subdivision listed under (2) communicating, for example, is impaired verbal communication. It does not indicate the cause, which, like many other patterns in the system, depends on the particular medical diagnosis, but could be related to either psychological or physical factors.

Figure 5.1 lists the NANDA nursing diagnosis categories as of 1992 (Schultz & Videbeck, 1994). The figure shows that most of the subdivisions under the patterns not already mentioned can have psychological and behavioral implications. The nursing profession developed these categories, it must be remembered, as a supplement rather than a substitute for medical diagnosis. It would be useful, however, to consider whether these categories are inclusive enough so that it would be possible to consider developing psychological interventions for the issues stated rather than to continue to use the current, overly broad psychiatric diagnosis system. The system is, after all, focused on the practical treatment interventions that nurses can make.

In 1982, Janet Williams and Holly Wilson, a nurse formerly critical of the *DSM* system, wrote an article that attempted to demonstrate the value of *DSM-III* for nurses. They lauded the multiaxial
aspects of *DSM-III* (current at the time) and suggested that nursing
concerns could be alleviated by the possible future incorporation
into the *DSM*s of an axis VI,

> one that would provide clinicians from diverse schools of thought
> or theoretical perspectives both within and among mental health
> disciplines with the opportunity to assess a client's problem in
> such a way as to explicitly direct a treatment or care plan. When
> it comes to transforming a DSM-III diagnosis into a plan of care,
> behaviorists, milieu therapists, analysts, social workers, psychol-
> ogists and nurses must make a supplemental treatment-related
> assessment. (Williams & Wilson, 1982, p. 20)

In response to Williams and Wilson's suggestion, Morrison,
Fisher, Wilson, and Underwood (1985) proposed just such an axis,
a Nursing Adaptation Evaluation. The first digit would reflect the
patient's current functioning on a scale from 1 to 4 (most to least).
The remaining five digits would code functioning in five areas in
which nursing provides care: nutrition, solitude and social interaction, grooming, activity (rest), and elimination, also rated on scales
from 1 to 4. The authors suggest that the assessment be made when
the patient is admitted to the hospital and again when discharged
to provide indications of progress as well as information for planning of follow-up services. I have no information of how fully this
axis was considered for inclusion in *DSM-IV*, but in any event it did
not survive to the final published version, possibly because its suggested dimensions were less psychologically oriented than the
NANDA diagnoses themselves.

A SUPPLEMENTAL SYSTEM FROM SOCIAL WORK: PIE

Reacting much as psychologists did, social workers realized that
insight from their unique perspective has not been included in the
DSM-III (Karls & Wandrei, 1992). Their organization decided to
develop a separate system for classifying the problems that are the
primary focus of social work. They wanted their system to provide:

> common language for all social work practitioners in all set-
> tings for describing their clients' problems
> a common capsulated description of social phenomena that

FIGURE 5.1. Nursing Diagnoses

PATTERN 1: EXCHANGING

	1.1.2.1	Altered Nutrition: More than Body Requirements
	1.1.2.2	Altered Nutrition: Less than Body Requirements
	1.1.2.3	Altered Nutrition: Potential for More than Body Requirements
*	1.2.1.1	Risk for Infection
*	1.2.2.1	Risk for Altered Body Temperature
	1.2.2.2	Hypothermia
	1.2.2.3	Hyperthermia
	1.2.2.4	Ineffective Thermoregulation
	1.2.3.1	Dysreflexia
	1.3.1.1	Constipation
	1.3.1.1.1	Perceived Constipation
	1.3.1.1.2	Colonic Constipation
	1.3.1.2	Diarrhea
	1.3.1.3	Bowel Incontinence
	1.3.2	Altered Urinary Elimination
	1.3.2.1.1	Stress Incontinence
	1.3.2.1.2	Reflex Incontinence
	1.3.2.1.3	Urge Incontinence
	1.3.2.1.4	Functional Incontinence
	1.3.2.1.5	Total Incontinence
	1.3.2.2	Urinary Retention
	1.4.1.1	Altered (Specify Type) Tissue Perfusion (Renal, Cerebral, Cardiopulmonary, Gastrointestinal, Peripheral)
	1.4.1.2.1	Fluid Volume Excess
	1.4.1.2.2.1	Fluid Volume Deficit
	1.4.1.2.2.2	Risk for Fluid Volume Deficit
*	1.4.2.1	Decreased Cardiac Output
	1.5.1.1	Impaired Gas Exchange
	1.5.1.2	Ineffective Airway Clearance
	1.5.1.3	Ineffective Breathing Pattern
	1.5.1.3.1	Inability to Sustain Spontaneous Ventilation
	1.5.1.3.2	Dysfunctional Ventilatory Weaning Response (DVWR)
*	1.6.1	Risk for Injury
	1.6.1.1	Risk for Suffocation
*	1.6.1.2	Risk for Poisoning
*	1.6.1.3	Risk for Trauma
*	1.6.1.4	Risk for Aspiration
*	1.6.1.5	Risk for Disuse Syndrome
	1.6.2	Altered Protection
	1.6.2.1	Impaired Tissue Integrity
	1.6.2.1.1	Altered Oral Mucous Membrane
	1.6.2.1.2.1	Impaired Skin Integrity
*	1.6.2.1.2.2	Risk for Impaired Skin Integrity
#	1.7.1	Decreased Adaptive Capacity: Intracranial
#	1.8	Energy Field Disturbance

PATTERN 2: COMMUNICATING

	2.1.1.1	Impaired Verbal Communication

PATTERN 3: RELATING

	3.1.1	Impaired Social Interaction
	3.1.2	Social Isolation
#	3.1.3	Risk for Loneliness
	3.2.1	Altered Role Performance
	3.2.1.1.1	Altered Parenting
	3.2.1.1.2	Risk for Altered Parenting
*	3.2.1.1.2.1	Risk for Altered Parent/Infant/Child Attachment
	3.2.1.2.1	Sexual Dysfunction
#	3.2.2	Altered Family Processes
	3.2.2.1	Caregiver Role Strain
*	3.2.2.2	Risk for Caregiver Role Strain
#	3.2.2.3.1	Altered Family Process: Alcoholism
	3.2.3.1	Parental Role Conflict
	3.3	Altered Sexuality Patterns

PATTERN 4: VALUING

	4.1.1	Spiritual Distress (Distress of the Human Spirit)
#	4.2	Potential for Enhanced Spiritual Well-Being

PATTERN 5: CHOOSING

	5.1.1.1	Ineffective Individual Coping
	5.1.1.1.1	Impaired Adjustment
	5.1.1.1.2	Defensive Coping
	5.1.1.1.3	Ineffective Denial
	5.1.2.1.1	Ineffective Family Coping: Disabling
	5.1.2.1.2	Ineffective Family Coping: Compromised
	5.1.2.2	Family Coping: Potential for Growth

FIGURE 5.1. (cont.)

#	5.1.3.1	Potential for Enhanced Community Coping
#	5.1.3.2	Ineffective Community Coping
	5.2.1	Ineffective Management of Therapeutic Regimen (Individuals)
	5.2.1.1	Noncompliance (Specify)
#	5.2.2	Ineffective Mangement of Therapeutic Regimen: Families
#	5.2.3	Ineffective Management of Therapeutic Regimen: Community
#	5.2.4	Ineffective Management of Therapeutic Regimen: Individual
	5.3.1.1	Decisional Conflict (Specify)
	5.4	Health Seeking Behaviors (Specify)

PATTERN 6: MOVING

	6.1.1.1	Impaired Physical Mobility
*	6.1.1.1.1	Risk for Peripheral Neurovascular Dysfunction
#	6.1.1.1.2	Risk for Perioperative Positioning Injury
	6.1.1.2	Activity Intolerance
	6.1.1.2.1	Fatigue
	6.1.1.3	Risk for Activity Intolerance
*	6.2.1	Sleep Pattern Disturbance
	6.3.1.1	Diversional Activity Deficit
	6.4.1.1	Impaired Home Maintenance Management
	6.4.2	Altered Health Maintenance
	6.5.1	Feeding Self Care Deficit
	6.5.1.1	Impaired Swallowing
	6.5.1.2	Ineffective Breastfeeding
	6.5.1.2.1	Interrupted Breastfeeding
	6.5.1.3	Effective Breastfeeding
	6.5.1.4	Ineffective Infant Feeding Pattern
	6.5.2	Bathing/Hygiene Self Care Deficit
	6.5.3	Dressing/Grooming Self Care Deficit
	6.5.4	Toileting Self Care Deficit
	6.6	Altered Growth and Development
	6.7	Relocation Stress Syndrome
#	6.8.1	Risk for Disorganized Infant Behavior
#	6.8.2	Disorganized Infant Behavior
#	6.8.3	Potential for Enhanced Organized Infant Behavior

PATTERN 7: PERCEIVING

7.1.1	Body Image Disturbance
7.1.2	Self Esteem Disturbance
7.1.2.1	Chronic Low Self Esteem
7.1.2.2	Situational Low Self Esteem
7.1.3	Personal Identity Disturbance
7.2	Sensory/Perceptual Alterations (Specify) (Visual, Auditory, Kinesthetic, Gustatory, Tactile, Olfactory)
7.2.1.1	Unilateral Neglect
7.3.1	Hopelessness
7.3.2	Powerlessness

PATTERN 8: KNOWING

	8.1.1	Knowledge Deficit (Specify)
#	8.2.1	Impaired Environmental Interpretation Syndrome
#	8.2.2	Acute Confusion
#	8.2.3	Chronic Confusion
	8.3	Altered Thought Processes
#	8.3.1	Impaired Memory

PATTERN 9: FEELING

	9.1.1	Pain
	9.1.1.1	Chronic Pain
	9.2.1.1	Dysfunctional Grieving
	9.2.1.2	Anticipatory Grieving
*	9.2.2	Risk for Violence: Self-Directed or Directed at Others
*	9.2.2.1	Risk for Self-Mutilation
	9.2.3	Post-Trauma Response
	9.2.3.1	Rape-Trauma Syndrome
	9.2.3.1.1	Rape-Trauma Syndrome: Compound Reaction
	9.2.3.1.2	Rape-Trauma Syndrome: Silent Reaction
	9.3.1	Anxiety
	9.3.2	Fear

Note: This list represents the NANDA-approved nursing diagnoses for clinical use and testing (1994). From *NANDA nursing diagnoses: Definitions and classification 1995–1996* (Philadelphia: North American Nursing Diagnosis Association, 1994).

#New diagnoses added in 1994 classified at level 1.4 using new Criteria for Staging.

*Diagnoses with modified label terminology in 1994. (This change was recommended by the NANDA Taxonomy Committee and adopted to remain consistent with the ICD.)

could facilitate treatment or amelioration of the problems presented by clients

a basis for gathering data required to measure the need for
services and to design human services programs and evaluate
effectiveness

a mechanism for clearer communication among social work
practitioners and between practitioners and administrators and
researchers

a basis for clarifying the domain of social work in the human
services field. (Karls & Wandrei, 1994a, p. 7)

Social work wished to develop a system that would be as atheoretical and as simple as possible. Their task force identified the concept
of social well-being as the basis upon which to build their classifications system. Calling their basic idea Person-In-Environment (PIE),
they describe human behavior as a result of intrapersonal and interpersonal forces in interaction. They saw these forces as originating
in "social performance expectations" arising out of an individual's
personal life experience or social context (see Figure 5.2).

PIE is a four-factor system. Factors I and II focus primarily on the
social functioning of an individual. Factor I, entitled Social Role
Problems, includes provision for listing various social roles, which
are grouped into four major categories: family roles, other interpersonal roles, occupational roles, and special life situation roles.
Under family roles are six subgroupings: parent, spouse, child, sib-
ling, other family, and significant other. Interpersonal roles include
lover, friend, neighbor, and other. Occupational roles include five
categories: worker—paid, worker—home, worker—volunteer, student, and other. The special life situations role subgroupings
include consumer, inpatient/client, outpatient/client, proba-
tioner/parolee, prisoner, immigrant—legal, immigrant—undocu-
mented, immigrant—refugee, and other. For all of these roles, nine
types of problems might arise, including power, ambivalence,
responsibility, dependency, loss, isolation, victimization, mixed,
and others. Each of these can be measured according to severity,
duration, and level of coping skills.

Factor II, entitled Environmental Problems, uses five subsys-
tems: economic, educational, legal, health, and social and affec-
tional. These also can be rated for severity and duration. Factor III,
Mental Disorders, is used to report diagnoses on axes I and II of the
DSM. Factor IV, entitled Physical Disorders, reports information
gathered from relevant medical sources (Karls & Wandrei, 1992).

FIGURE 5.2

Basic Structure of PIE

Factor I: Social Functioning Problems

A. Social role in which each problem is identified (four categories)
B. Type of problem in social role (nine types)
C. Severity of problem (6-point indicator)
D. Duration of problem (6-point indicator)
E. Ability of client to cope with problem

Factor II: Environmental Problems

A. Social system where each problem is identified (six systems)
B. Specific type of problem within each social system
   (number varies for each social system)
C. Severity of problem (6-point indicator)
D. Duration of problem

Factor III: Mental Health Problems

A. Clinical syndromes (Axis I of DSM-IV)
B. Personality and developmental disorders
   (Axis II of DSM-IV)

Factor IV: Physical Health Problems

A. Diseases diagnosed by a physician (Axis III of DSM-IV, ICD-9)
B. Other health problems reported by client and others

Source: Karls and Wandrei (1994a, p. 24).

As yet little literature is available on the application of this system, how widely used it is, or what its eventual usefulness is likely to be. Neither psychiatrists nor psychologists have yet heard of it, for the most part. It is problem oriented and it does not, in itself, label. It deals very explicitly with the context of the individual being diagnosed, without preconceived ideas about etiology. It is purely descriptive. I think it has a great deal of potential beyond the field of social work and would like to see it more widely used.

Social workers, in developing their system, very carefully avoided interfering in any way with the *DSMs*. They have, however, added an important dimension they noted to be nearly absent in the *DSMs* and have asserted an important claim to what they view as their domain. The PIE manual's appendix even lists possible social work interventions for interpersonal, environmental, and intrapsychic problems (Karls & Wandrei, 1994b).

PSYCHOLOGY SYSTEMS

The profession of psychology has made sporadic attempts to develop its own official classification system. For a variety of reasons, not least among them the vast scope of the subject and the difficulty of persuading different theoretical camps to agree, no attempt has gotten very far and most were quickly aborted. Some opinion papers generated from these attempts have been discussed earlier. The fact that the issue resurfaces regularly, however, is one indication that psychology is dissatisfied with the psychiatric *DSMs*. Psychologists in general have expressed the most displeasure with the lack of true operationalism and atheoreticality in the *DSMs*, although social workers Kirk and Kutchins (1992) demonstrated the fallacy in the use of reliability statistics in *DSM-III* and beyond.

To the best of my knowledge, only one person, Charles Downing (1983), has attempted by himself to formulate an alternative behavior classification system. He suggested using adaptability as the base. Components he suggested for inclusion were physical development, occupational expression, avocational expression, and interpersonal relationships. He considered that developmental tasks occur throughout life. Some of the ones he suggested were personal competency, personal sexual role identity, capacity for meaningful relationships, appropriate level of independence, personal purpose, and sense of integrity. In his view, maladaptive behavior was likely to result from the failure to accomplish appropriate developmental tasks, using grieving as an example.

I have not been able to find any literature that has followed up on Downing's ideas. At least two other systems that have some promise in the field of classification, however, have acquired adherents. One is the Five-Factor Model of Personality (FFM), which can be applied primarily to the personality disorders, although it may have relevance beyond this realm (Trull & Sher, 1994). The other is Lorna Smith Benjamin's Structural Analysis of Social Behavior (SASB), which has some possibility of encompassing the entire range of emotional disturbance.

Five-Factor Model of Personality (FFM)

The theoretical underpinnings of this model are not new. It is based on early work by McDougall and Thurstone on personality traits, but was brought into the current era by McCrae and John (1992) and Digman (1994). Much of the work on this model has been based on the interpretation of factor analyses, where personality is viewed in terms of five dimensions: neuroticism (N), extroversion (E), openness to experience (O), agreeableness (A), and conscientiousness (C) (Digman, 1994). Its proponents believe they have discovered the basic dimensions of personality and that it

> could provide a common language for psychologists from different traditions, a basic phenomenon for personality theorists to explain, a natural framework for organizing research, and a guide to the industrial/organizational, and clinical psychologists. (McCrae & John, 1992, p. 177)

Research has demonstrated that neuroticism is more closely related to personality dysfunction than any other. For none of the other traits does an extreme automatically imply a personality disorder. In addition, the relationship of axis I disorders to personality remains equally clouded (Widiger & Trull, 1992). The Five-Factor Model has a mathematical rather than individual basis and the information it yields about persons seems too limited to be useful clinically. What value it may have seems to be limited primarily to research.

Structural Analysis of Social Behavior (SASB)

This system has its roots in the theories of the neo-Freudians who focused on the interpersonal realm. Originally, the concept of interpersonal diagnosis was developed by Timothy Leary (1957), who developed the Interpersonal Circle, a circular array of behavior variables built around two axes (love–hate and dominance–submission). Using this and other related models, Lorna Smith Benjamin developed her model in 1974. Her system consists of three grids (see Figure 5.3); in each the horizontal axis is affiliation (love–hate) and the vertical axis is interdependence. The diamonds relate to three levels of functioning. Two relate to the interpersonal world, one focusing on view of others and the other view of self. The third applies to intrapsychic aspects of behaving. Assessment is made via self-report or report by significant others. Each spot on

FIGURE 5.3

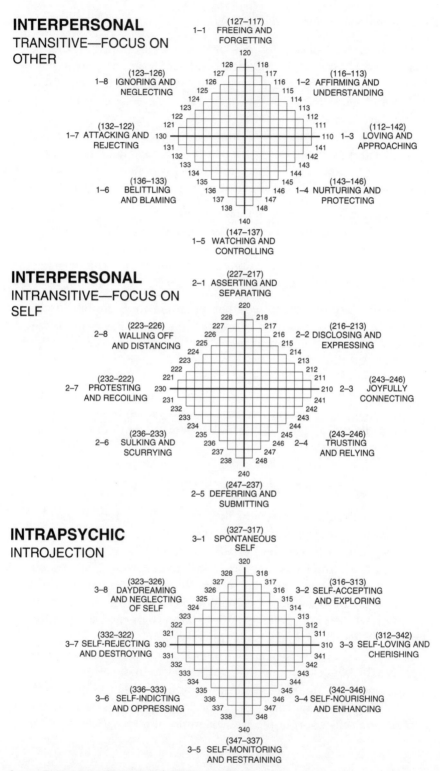

a grid represents a point somewhere on a dimension between two poles with a total of 108 categories possible. The long-form grid as shown can be collapsed into a shorter, less elaborate structure.

Benjamin, who functions as a clinician as well as academician, has been working on her system and accumulating data for over 25 years. She believes it has useful therapeutic applications and also has the capacity to deal in a somewhat dimensional fashion with the categories in the *DSM*s. Her work had some impact upon the descriptions of the axis II personality disorders in *DSM-IV* (Benjamin, 1994). Although feminists in general have not studied this system in detail, the idea of dimensionality rather than rigid categorization seems consonant with feminist thinking, and this system therefore seems potentially useful.

Relational Diagnosis

At the last moment of preparing this book, I came across yet another system for diagnosis now emerging (Kaslow, 1996). Still in its infancy, this system encompasses four broad categories of disorders: disorders of relationships, relationship problems associated with individual disorders, disorders that require relational data for their validity, and individual disorders whose evocation, course, and treatment are strongly influenced by relationship factors (Reiss, 1996). Proponents of this system come primarily from a family therapy background and have concluded that the *DSM-IV* is extremely limited when viewed from their perspective; this approach bears watching.

SYSTEMS USED IN OTHER COUNTRIES

As previously mentioned, the *DSM* system, as now represented by *DSM-IV*, has become the bible of the mental health and related establishments in the United States. Despite much dissatisfaction with the *DSM*s, few mental health workers have explored alternatives. By studying systems used in other countries and in professions other than psychiatry in our country, it should be possible to gain some perspective on some of the issues involved in conceptualization and categorization.

The nature of any system that classifies emotional, mental, psychological, psychiatric, or related problems is clearly related to how the groups involved conceptualize these processes. That is partly why I had to use so many alternative adjectives just now to describe this situation. It should be clear by now that our system in the United States is rooted in a broader European tradition. This should not be surprising, for a European tradition underpins much of our intellectual life. Nonetheless, the U.S. and European systems bear important differences, in part related to other differences in our ways of life. Kroll, for example, discusses some of the differences between us and the French:

> The philosophical foundations of American psychiatry are largely pragmatic, empirical, operational, inductive, anti-intellectual, Cartesian dualistic, and logical positivistic. By contrast, French psychiatry has been profoundly influenced by philosophical thinking that is speculative, existential, structuralistic, deductive, Cartesian monadic, and metaphysical. (Kroll, 1979, p. 1135)

The use of psychodynamic, organic, or behavioral formulations—or some combination of all three—fails to encompass all the possibilities for underlying assumptions. French systems, for example, at that time tended to emphasize existential angst rather than detailing syndromes and symptom entities. They focused on the subjective feelings of the individual (Kroll, 1979). The French have used a narrower definition of schizophrenia than we did prior to *DSM-III* and defined it as chronic. Other cases we would label as schizophrenic would probably fall into their categories of chronic hallucinatory psychosis and *bouffée délierante*, which is acute and in which symptoms quickly disappear (Pull, Pull, & Pichot, 1988).

Yet other systems used in different countries rely on a presumption of trauma as the basis for most mental disorders. In Denmark, for example, brief criminal psychotic states are attributed to "abnormal singular reaction" (Stromgren, 1988). Others focus on behavioral criteria, but in a manner different from our own (Stengel, 1959). As we move further from our direct intellectual forebears, differences become even more profound. The underpinnings of some societies' systems are spirituality and religion, which encompass what we consider to be in the personal, emotional realm. These systems may or may not qualify as mental health systems because what we might call ailments are administered to by spiritual rather than medical advisers.

African psychiatrists hold the view that marijuana can produce psychoses and/or precipitate latent psychoses. They are not primarily concerned with personality disorder diagnoses except in criminal cases where psychopathic personality may be diagnosed. They dispute among themselves as to the existence of excitement states that quickly remit. They also find that depression occurs in their population in somatic or bodily complaints rather than including a sense of guilt (Binitie, 1988).

Other classification and diagnostic systems are not as fully delineated and systematized as they are in the *DSM*s. One result of this difference is that our system, in an era of growing internationalism, has become one of the greatest influences on the development of classification elsewhere. Since 1948, the World Health Organization has published and regularly revised an International Classification of Diseases, which includes both physical as well as psychiatric disorders, and asked its member nations to use it in reporting statistics on mental illness. One major reason for having such a uniform system is to gather reliable statistics so that we can answer more definitively than we can now questions about whether the rates of psychosis or depression are similar in different countries.

In the United States, since the 1950s, the American Psychiatric Association *DSM*s have existed in a very uneasy relationship to the international system. They have differed from one another in different ways at different times. There has been pressure toward making the *DSM*s conform to the ICD, and equal pressure pushing the ICD in the direction of our categorizations. The largest differences, however, have seemed to occur more in how different categories are used than in the broad overarching categories themselves.

On the other hand, Maser, Kaelber, and Weise (1991) reported that a survey of clinicians in 42 countries revealed that they prefer the American *DSM*s to the ICD. They also reported that many new features of *DSM-III* have been incorporated into the ICD–10. They go so far as to suggest *DSM-V* perhaps may never need to be published and that in the future the ICD may become the world as well as American standard. They make the analogy to cities or states enacting innovative legislation that may later be enacted nationally. All of this seems to be their opinions only, since their own data strongly suggest that the American *DSM*s have become a world standard rather than the ICD. Mezzich, Fabrega, Mezzich, and Coffman (1985) had earlier found that *DSM-III* was used almost as much as the ICD–9 in 52 countries spanning all continents. In their survey, Africa was the only region where the *DSM* was not seen as particularly useful.

Some 75% of the world's psychiatric diagnoses occur in the less developed countries (Mezzich & von Cranach, 1988). Where these countries do have psychiatric services separate from medical services, it is likely that their psychiatrists were trained in the United States. This has spread the influence of our *DSMs* around the world, although they were never designed to encompass culture-specific disorders that exist in some parts of the world. This is especially true in the area of acute or transient psychoses, which are generally rapid in onset, have a short duration, and are generally followed by complete recovery. In many of these cases, the content of delusional thinking, if it occurs, is closely related to the religious and/or spiritual beliefs of the specific cultural group and is not parallel to anything other than atypical psychosis in our *DSMs* (Wig & Parhee, 1988).

Haghighat (1994) has pointed out ways in which even the ICD–10 falls short in the area of cultural sensitivity. He referred to the huge immigration into the United States of peoples from vastly different cultural backgrounds and suggested that *DSM-III-R* (this equally applies to *DSM-IV*) has pitfalls for dealing with these populations. Among specific examples, he referred to the changes in the ability to keep or find a job, used diagnostically in the *DSMs* but subject to large cross-cultural differences. He also mentioned mispronunciation of words, which has to be related to one's subculture before a child can be diagnosed with speech articulation disorder. He also indicated that the criteria for pica (another children's diagnosis) do not provide for culturally sanctioned practices in religious rituals. Additionally, he also discussed the issue of independent living by the elderly, which also varies considerably cross-culturally, and how that is to be considered from a diagnostic point of view. One of his examples is especially relevant for women: the age when girl children marry or are sexually available. While Western cultures disapprove of marriages between adult males and underage girl children, in Nepal, for example, girls are usually married by the age of fourteen. Haghighat also pointed out that overdoses and anorexia nervosa, which occur mainly in the West and not elsewhere, are as culture-specific as any other diagnoses that are listed as such.

A British Example: The Foulds Hierarchy of Personal Illness

Although other alternative systems have been developed in other countries, the Foulds hierarchy is included here because it is based on entirely different concepts than the American *DSMs*.

This is a conceptually based system developed by Graham Foulds and his colleagues. To date, it has not been adopted anywhere as an official classification system, but it has been much discussed in the British psychiatric literature.

Foulds (1976) defined personal illness as involving

> some loss of the ability to intend one's own actions in a way which is usually consonant with the intentions of others. This change in relationship must comprise a change in attitude and accompanying affect. States of anxiety or of depression—with or without symptoms—are, as it were, an acknowledgement that this adverse change has got under way or is imminent. (p. 9)

He called his system a hierarchy both because four classes of disorder are arranged in accord with increasing severity of disturbance and because it is assumed that symptoms associated with classes lower in the system will always be present when higher level (i.e., more severe) disorders are seen.

Class 1 is labeled dysthymic states (DS) and refers to changes in affect. Foulds thought these were common to most psychiatric patients. There are three types: states of anxiety (sA), states of depression (sD), and states of elation (sE).

Class 2 is neurotic symptoms (NS). Its characteristic feature is that the behavior is viewed by the person as alien to his or her normal self (what would be called ego-dystonic in psychoanalytic terminology). It contains five groups: dissociative symptoms (Ds), conversion symptoms (CVs), phobic symptoms (Ps), compulsive symptoms (CPs), and ruminative symptoms (Rs).

Class 3 is called integrated delusions (ID). It comprises individuals whose perceptions of reality and self are grossly distorted and changed from their usual self. There are three groups: delusions of persecution (dP), delusions of grandeur (dG), and delusions of contrition (dC).

Class 4 is delusions of disintegration (DD). In this, the person has lost perception of his or her own self as the agent of actions, feelings, and thoughts. It is not differentiated into subgroups.

Foulds was dissatisfied with the inability of most classification systems to describe the shifting symptom patterns of most psychiatric illnesses. He also thought his system would lead to more appropriate treatment decisions. Affective symptoms are viewed as low-level phenomena, and when they reach psychotic proportions, the psychosis is the most important aspect. Some subtypes of schizophrenia are in class 4, although others fall in class 3. Morey (1987) reported favorably on the research that has been done on various aspects of this classification scheme.

SUMMARY

It is perhaps worth recapitulating some aspects from the discussion of the purposes of diagnosis that were discussed earlier. Feminist therapists make strong efforts to deal with women within the broadest possible conceptualization of their lives. In the next chapter, I describe what I think the etiological stew must look like when that is done. This is, however, for the most part, useful at a theoretical and research level rather than a clinical level.

Of the systems I have described, I think that the Structural Analysis of Social Behavior has a great deal of potential to be clinically useful. However, I am even more impressed with social work's Person-In-Environment system. This is primarily because it is very concrete, clinically directed and oriented toward possible behavioral interventions, and conveys the context in which the person lives. The same may be said of the new relational diagnostic concept that has only barely emerged at present. Because it appears to have a significant potential to encompass context—especially relationship context, which all too frequently has been ignored—those of us who think that diagnosis must be contextually focused will be watching this new development closely.

## CHAPTER 6

What Is Normal Anyway?
Issues in Categorization

WHAT IS A MENTAL DISORDER?

WHEN WE PONDER what to include in a classification system for mental or emotional problems, an easy path to take is to include those that have been recognized over the centuries and hope that they are still useful (McReynolds, 1989). As we have already seen, however, this consensus can be either flatly wrong or conditionally wrong within a particular context. It is highly likely to be one-sided, moreover, when applied to women.

Another possible avenue is to consider personal views of distress. Here, we have to ask if distress is automatically equal to abnormality. Society generally attributes disturbance to many persons who do not consider themselves to have anything wrong with them at all. This occurs often with people labeled schizophrenic. The role of subjective feelings of distress is complex both at the level of formulating diagnostic systems and at the individual level, where some particular person is being labeled.

Perhaps the question "What is a mental illness" cannot ever be definitively answered. Let us begin with the definition used in *DSM-IV,* one that is essentially unchanged from *DSM-III:*

> [It is] conceptualized as a clinically significant behavioral or psychological syndrome or pattern that occurs in an individual and that is associated with present distress (e.g., a painful symptom) or disability (i.e., impairment in one or more important areas of

functioning) or with a significantly increased risk of suffering death, pain, disability, or an important loss of freedom. In addition, this syndrome or pattern must not be merely an expectable and culturally sanctioned response to a particular event, for example, the death of a loved one. Whatever its original cause, it must currently be considered a manifestation of a behavioral, psychological, or biological dysfunction in the individual. Neither deviant behavior (e.g., political, religious, or sexual) nor conflicts that are primarily between the individual and society are mental disorders unless the deviance or conflict is a symptom of dysfunction in the individual, as described above. (American Psychiatric Association, 1994, pp. xxi–xxii)

The key words are *distress* and *disability*, but the definition fails to recognize the role of outside judgment in deciding what a disability is or how serious distress or disability has to be before it is labeled a mental disorder. Interestingly enough, by including the idea that it is associated with "an important loss of freedom," the definition could logically encompass all criminal behavior, although this is not mentioned elsewhere in the manual. Implicit also in the same phrase is the idea of social approbation as one sign of mental disorder—without, of course, mentioning who disapproves of whom.

Widiger and Trull (1991) formulated a definition that essentially agrees with the formal one in the *DSMs* but that also accords well with the clinical subculture in which we informally label each other crazy all the time. It does not, however, deal with just how one would formulate a classification scheme. For Widiger and Trull:

A mental disorder is essentially an involuntary, organismic impairment in psychological functioning (i.e., cognitive, affective and/or behavioral). Persons who are hindered in their ability to adapt flexibly to stress, to make optimal life decisions, to fulfill desired potentials, or to sustain meaningful or satisfying relationships as a result of an impairment in cognitive, affective, and/or behavioral functioning over which they have insufficient control, have a mental disorder. This definition includes many conditions considered by others to represent simply problems in living. Many mental disorders are minor and inconsequential (e.g., inhibitions and anxieties), just as many physical disorders (e.g., colds, cuts and hay fever). Everyone goes through life suffering from and/or tolerating a variety of mental disorders, some of which are chronic (e.g., personality disorders), just as everyone suffers and/or tolerates a variety of physical disorders, some of which are chronic (e.g., myopia). The extent to which any particular person is mentally ill is only a matter of degree, type, and time of life. (p. 112)

This relativistic definition encompasses most of us. It still, however, locates the disorder in the individual, not recognizing that anything from outside could possibly influence the person's ability to function in any sphere. The authors implicitly recognize context only in describing a person with a fear of heights who could not look out the window of a tall building or fly in an airplane but who lived in a small town and had no need to fly. However, they would label such a person as having a mental disorder "analogous to a silent disease that requires additional (potentiating) conditions to manifest the overt symptomatology" (p. 112).

Walter Gove (1980) excluded alcoholism and drug abuse, acute and chronic brain syndromes, mental retardation, and personality disorders from his definition of mental illness. The key aspects of his definition were personal distress and psychotic disorganization. He used these in pursuing an answer to the question of whether the apparent higher mental illness rates for women were an artifact of clinician or patient behavior. Marilyn Johnson (1980) challenged his definition because it specifically excluded the categories men were more likely to fall under. She pointed out that under his definition, a beaten wife might be diagnosed as mentally ill (e.g., depressed) while the husband would not.

Gove's definition, though not in official use, illustrates some of the many problems in this arena. Many others have attempted definitions. I include his because of the concern in the early 1980s in the question of relative mental disorder rates for males and females, a concern that seems to have dissipated over time, perhaps because of increased awareness of the problems inherent in the very definition of the mental illness or mental disorder.

Cooper (1988) suggested that psychiatry will remain vulnerable to arguments that "disease" can be used to denote any phenomenon thought to be undesirable until it can actually define what is meant by mental illness. He proposed that psychiatry give up the attempt at definition and concede that its classifications are neither diseases nor disorders but simply the problems that psychiatrists are currently consulted about.

The fuzziness associated with the problem of definition is analogous to that of intelligence testing, wherein intelligence is defined as what intelligence tests measure. A mental disorder is what some official body decides it is. Please note that I am not implying that distress and disability do not exist. I am merely indicating that the degree of individual emotional turmoil is a matter quite separate from the formal process of diagnosis.

Kendell (1988) tells us that:

> Our classifications, categories and definitions are unstable not because psychiatrists are particularly argumentative, fickle, or indecisive, but because we do not yet understand the etiology of the majority of disorders we study and treat, and because the clusters of symptoms that we identify as characteristic of different syndromes merge imperceptibly into one another. (p. 336)

THE BASES OF CLASSIFICATION

We need to remind ourselves that the formal process of classification began with the need to have an inventory or census of persons who were hospitalized. With the purported purpose of relating diagnosis more appropriately to treatment, our present system has evolved into a rigid set of categories, whose existence serves the needs of our massive and cumbersome medical reimbursement and legal systems more than it does the therapeutic needs of patients or clients—or even clinicians for that matter. If we accept the assumption that establishing classifications into which we can fit all mental and emotional disturbances is at all a worthy enterprise, the next question has to be what such a system should be based on.

In the absence of theoretical predispositions, the most obvious way to classify people is on the basis of their symptoms. To a great extent, this is what the history of mental illness tells us was actually done as the field began. Very soon, however, it became apparent that similar symptomatology—say, confusion—could be seen where you knew that someone has suffered a severe blow to the head and when you could verify that nothing serious like that had ever happened to another individual. In an example like this, we can see the start of interest in etiology.

Internationally, probably the major disagreement in diagnostic classification is whether disorders should be categorized on the basis of etiology or symptomatology (Stengel, 1959). No system is purely based on either, but the relative weights given to one or the other have varied over a wide range. Although these two concepts have been the most usual bases for mental health classification, they do not exhaust all the possibilities. Let us consider some of the possibilities that have been proposed and used in various times and places.

Classification According to Symptoms

In general, except at the extreme pathology end of the continuum, classifying according to symptoms has proven difficult. It seems that almost every behavior that looks like a symptom may not differentiate one entity from another, and, since similar behaviors may mask differences in meaning, it must be viewed in accord with the particular meaning it has for the particular individual. Further, cultural perceptions and expectations greatly influence what may legitimately be called a symptom (Linton, 1956). Nevertheless, every diagnostic system has to some degree incorporated this approach. It shows up, of course, in the *DSMs*, including *DSM-IV*, where it still exists.

Class of Behaviors

Stengel (1959) discussed the idea of assigning a classification name to particular groups of symptoms or behaviors rather than dealing with the problems of whether they represent a disease entity or originate in another etiology. In the official classification, this has probably been done more than anyone would like to acknowledge because of the difficulty in reliably establishing etiology, although it is not generally acknowledged or well accepted as a classification strategy. As with classification according to symptoms, it is generally regarded as a conceptually low-level way of determining diagnostic entities.

Prognosis

To some extent, this criterion is built into many diagnostic systems. Take psychosis and neurosis, for example. The prognosis for patients at the psychotic end of the continuum is generally thought to be poor; at what used to be called the neurotic end of the continuum, the patient's prognosis, at least in theory, is good. For some practitioners, if psychotic individuals get well, it demonstrates that they did not suffer from schizophrenia in the first place.

Prognosis is the basis for axis II in the present American system, in that traits diagnosed here are considered of long standing and not easily reversible. An axis II diagnosis suggests that behavior is highly likely to be permanent and the expectation that it will continue. Although they are not axis II diagnoses, this expectation follows the schizophrenic diagnoses as well, although it is less well established for the bipolar conditions.

THE DIAGNOSIS OF PATHOLOGY

Psychoanalysis has postulated that emotional and mental disorders generally happen as a result of failures in the progress of psychosexual development. Not so well recognized, however, it also strongly implies that the foundation of this progress is genetic, which may strongly determine its outcomes in ill-defined ways. The discovery in the early twentieth century that a tertiary result of untreated syphilis was general paresis, an organically based mental disorder, encouraged those who sought purely organic bases for all mental illness. Others have argued for an etiology based solely on environmental factors (Jacobs, 1994).

Our exploration of factors here will not deal in the dichotomies that have so often characterized discussion of this subject. Rather, etiology will be discussed in terms of how the individual is affected as a physical entity, how external events impact upon the individual physically as well as psychologically, how society views the individual (and conversely, the individual views society), and the impact of larger cultural differences. The influence of the examiner, the individual who has the authority to issue diagnoses and attach the label, will also be discussed. This last is not the least of the factors that need to be considered, although it is formally included in the mix only rarely.

The Individual

The first influence is genetic makeup. Many individuals over a long time span have suggested or implied that this is the locus of all or most psychological difficulties, although conclusive research findings have not supported their claims. While many attempts have been made to identify, for example, a gene for schizophrenia, these attempts have usually been clouded with controversy and disputed when they are publicized. We do know with some degree of certainty, of course, that genetic makeup contributes to intellectual development and ability, although we are uncertain about how much, and that intelligence plays some part in personality development and the learning of social skills. Beyond this point, we are not able to fully ascertain that all or even most intellectual development is genetic. As of now, our knowledge about intellect remains sketchy and partial—and it is even more so in the area of mental disorders. While we may suspect that there are strong genetic components to the development of mental disorders, we cannot yet confirm this with any degree of authority or unanimity. The lack of supporting data has not, however, deterred some individuals from continuing to assert that bad genes ultimately cause mental ills.

The next possible physical influence is the uterine environment. Here, chemical substances in the mother's body can result in gross physical and mental abnormalities (Thalidomide babies, for example), and uterine events can trigger anomalies of development. But again we are not far enough along to identify less overt or more subtle effects. Except for major widespread events (Thalidomide, again), these effects have not been explored. An example is fetal alcohol syndrome, which is attributed not to genetics but to alcohol flowing into the baby's bloodstream from the mother, potentially retarding intellectual development and causing other abnormalities, including signs of alcohol withdrawal in the infant.

As we consider the circumstances after birth, the possibilities become even more complex, even if we stick to the realm of strict physical causation. We have identified some mental states that can be directly caused by physical ailments of different sorts. Possible examples include depressive mood, which is physiologically related to untreated diabetes or to some heart ailments. Even here, there is not full agreement. To repeat, we know little about subtle effects such as those that might be related, say, to variations in the production of internal endorphins, hormones, or even pheromones or other chemicals within a given individual.

Just as fetal alcohol syndrome results from ingested substances, the modern world has laid us open to a wide range of effects, still unstudied, of chemical substances that can be ingested later in life. There is much dispute yet about the physical effects of the industrial pollution in which most of us live. The mental and emotional effects have barely been reported.

In the interest of completeness, the effects of voluntarily ingested substances, whether alcohol, street drugs, or medication that is prescribed or taken without prescription, also have to be mentioned. Studies indicate that psychotropic medication given for the psychotic disorders has long-term biological effects (Breggin, 1990), which have also mostly been ignored. In my own professional experience, some portion of the difficulties in recent patients with major mental disorders may be attributable to the lingering effects of major long-term use of street drugs. This also does not seem to have been well studied as yet.

Another aspect of the physical realm to be considered is even more subtle: that related to emotional rather than physical interactivity with the external world. We are beginning to know that certain kinds of traumatic events may permanently alter significant aspects of a person's nervous system and that reaction to trauma is therefore not solely a psychological phenomenon. For anyone surprised by this, consider the fact, well known for a long time, that children raised without language spoken to them and instruction in language given to them at an appropriate time cannot later learn to speak and to understand human language. In a process analogous to imprinting in the lower animals, something happens to the brain in such cases so that what we ordinarily consider to be psychological (i.e., not physically caused) results can no longer take place. It is possible that many more types of events have this kind of interactive effect on the nervous system than we currently know. We can conceptualize this as a significant factor, especially for those who have grown up in psychologically deprived and abusive environments (van der Kolk, Greenberg, Boyd, & Krystal, 1985).

Yet another factor to consider is the role of physical ailments as psychological stressors. How patients perceive their symptoms and conceptualize their vulnerability play a part here. Cohen and Rodriguez (1995) tell us that reactions can include catastrophizing, perfectionism, and self-blame. These in turn can increase stress and decrease perceptions of control and self-esteem, altering the person's behaviors and the nature of relationships with others, primarily because of mood and anxiety disorders.

Interrelationships with People

Implied in what has already been said is an axiom that human beings, especially young human beings, need other people and what they can offer psychologically. We can point, tragically, to infantile miasma, or wasting away due to the lack of interpersonal contact with a primary caretaker even when physical needs are met.

The nature of relationships with early caretakers, whether seen in psychoanalytic terms or otherwise, has to be significant in emotional and psychological development. Erikson saw this as the period when basic trust in other people either is or is not developed and postulates that this underlies and affects all the later stages of psychological growth. If the initial foundation stone is not present, the remainder of the edifice of personality remains shaky at best. Whether this theoretical viewpoint is accepted or not, the underlying point remains that humans need other people and this need is probably significant for psychological development.

I have separated this from the influence of specific traumas (see the next section). Clearly, though, abuse of whatever kind from a significant caretaker is qualitatively different from abuse from a stranger. Although we intuit that later abusive relationships are even more devastating when they are built on earlier abusive ones, we still have relatively little firm data about these effects except that we know that significant psychological symptomatology often results.

We must not ignore, either, the effects of children on their caretakers. Children differ in myriad ways from birth. Measurements have been made for such characteristics as activity level, autonomic reactivity, behavioral inhibition, sociability, and the like. Research easily supports the idea that such factors as these influence how other people react to individual children. If a child is emotionally or physically difficult in any way, this is often reflected in parental behavior (Rutter, 1987). At this point we can only speculate about the results of such mutually unsatisfactory interactive behavior.

Events

As we begin to think about the long parade of events that occur daily in the life of each individual, we have to deal with several different ways they influence behavior. Psychoanalytic theory postulates that some kinds of events result in conflict and later maladjustment. Although relatively little research supports many of these notions, they persist (Lerman, 1986). Every psychological theory of development postulates that later behavior is somehow related to events, particularly those that take place in childhood and the developmental years. The problem is that theories differ on which events result in which consequences (Kagan, 1984).

A growing body of evidence has been accumulating in the past

10 to 15 years that specifically implicates trauma, particularly sexual and physical abuse during one's formative years, in the development of a wide variety of emotional and mental ills in later years. One problem here is that we do not have any direct correspondence between the type of trauma experienced and the kind of mental problems and symptomatology developed later, although van der Kolk (personal communication, December 9, 1990) has suggested some differences between the effects of active abuse and those of neglect and deprivation. While we know that severe physical and sexual trauma happens to males as well as females, we also know that it happens significantly more often to girls and women of all ages.

In addition to developmental trauma, trauma such as that experienced in major general disasters such as wars and other catastrophes, as well as individual trauma such as rape and other violence to one's person at any age, clearly has the strong possibility of triggering emotional distress and persistent behaviors that can be labeled abnormal (Terr, 1983, 1991).

The subject of events, if that is what we call experience, is, however, broader yet. It is worth noting that hospitalized people, particularly those hospitalized for long periods, look and act differently from the general population and are likely to be less than typically responsive to events and other people. Some people have conceptualized this as the end point of schizophrenia, but it appears in persons with all types of diagnoses and is rarely treated (Zusman, 1973). The phenomenon occurs for a variety of reasons, with long-term hospitalization itself being one of them. The various experiences associated with hospitalization, the forms of debasement and devaluation that are part and parcel of such experiences, are events that become embedded in individual psyches. These people need help that, unfortunately, is rarely available.

In a study that paralleled the well-known one by Rosenhan (1973) but included the accounts of the "patients" themselves, Goldman, Bohr, and Steinberg (1973) described the stays of two of the authors, one on an admissions ward and the other on a ward for more chronic patients. Among the phenomena they experienced was that of betrayal—fear that they would be forgotten by friends and relatives. They suggested that their feelings paralleled those of patients and were situationally induced by the impersonalization they experienced. Information about length of stay (indefinite) given at admission also was involved. They also mentioned boredom, which resulted in minor events taking on huge importance and their dependency on the staff for even minor matters. In many ways, what they report parallels accounts of internment in concentration camps, hostage situations, and prison.

At yet another level, but possible to see also under the general heading of events, are the victimization and poverty that individuals of lesser education, lower income, low socioeconomic status, and unemployment experience. In accord with the mechanisms suggested by Landrine et al. (1995), the fact that women may suffer these proportionately more often than men may relate to women being at greater risk for depression, a frequent consequence of these experiences (McGrath, Keita, Strickland, & Russo, 1990).

Society

Some traumas exist in other than direct physical form and so are noted here rather than earlier. Social judgments about behavior, for instance, influence people to judge themselves and have effects similar in many ways to physical trauma. Examples are verbal abuse of children; negative judgments about sexual orientation or particular sexual behavior; degrading attitudes and comments about gender, ethnicity, and/or race; implicit and explicit direction about what is considered to be appropriate for one's gender, race, class, and so on; and sanctions imposed against those who deviate.

One historical example of society's influence is masturbation. Freud declared masturbation to be a direct cause of some neuroses, postulating this as using up a finite amount of sexual energy. He failed to recognize that in his day, masturbation was generally regarded as negative and sometimes evil, mostly but not entirely on a religious basis. Men and women regularly heard about the negative consequences of masturbation from parents, school, church, and other authorities. People suffered severe neurotic symptoms apparently as a direct result of masturbation, but more accurately as a result of their internalized view of society's value judgments. In our day, on the other hand, it is rare to see someone who comes to believe he or she is bad or inherently disturbed because of masturbation. Indeed, masturbation is often now promoted as a way to improve sexual experience. Even if that message is not incorporated, the manifestly negative messages have largely disappeared. It is not now generally considered to cause disordered behavior, and so for the most part it does not. This example suggests that societal stigmas rather than behavior itself may play a significant role in how individuals react.

For the most part, any concern with how general societal views impinge on an individual's self view has been only peripherally reflected in official schemas. When it comes to social views of the appropriate role for women, the psychiatric establishment, particularly the proponents of psychoanalytic theory, has to answer for much of the psychological distress and internalized judgments imposed on women over some 75 years until the feminist movement developed enough of a consensus to propose meaningful alternatives.

Cultural Differences

This area leads us back into the question of what normality is and whether it is possible to define it in a way that transcends a particular culture and thus does not reside in any particular behavior. Some general definitions exist (Offer & Sabshin, 1974), although in most instances, we know that symptoms seem to be strongly affected by the individual's cultural milieu (Linton, 1956). Cultural anthropologists have been telling us this for a long time, but their message has not been grasped outside their field, although Ralph Linton differentiated between relative and absolute normality. He suggested that some abnormalities had a physiological basis and the individuals manifesting them would be abnormal in any society, although their symptoms might differ and others might depend on the norms of a given culture. Later anthropological writing takes a similar view. Psychosis has been identified as existing in most cultures (Murphy, 1978).

Freud's definition of mental health, to love well and to work well, is suitably global. However, the specific details he mentioned relate to a specific cultural milieu without any apparent awareness on his part that they were culturally bound. Cultural specifics were incorporated into psychoanalytic theory as if they were actually universally true. We have discussed Freud's view of masturbation. Additional themes such as the Oedipal complex and penis envy, which are directly relevant to our topic, were also dealt with similarly (Lerman, 1986).

Erik Erikson's implied definition—to pass through all his developmental stages satisfactorily—has to be looked at in terms of whether his stages are culturally determined or indeed are universal. Cultural critics argue that Western society promotes the idea of individuality and autonomy in ways other societies do not, societies where collective and family cohesion is more important. Since the development of autonomy is an important stage in Erikson's system, his definition does not stand when we look at it in this light.

Although it is difficult to formulate a general definition, we know that the process of diagnosis implicitly compares any given behavior to a standard of normality. This has been true throughout the development of the *DSM*s. In the workaday world, knowledge and even awareness of how cultural differences play a part in what is assumed to be the standard are minimal. *DSM-IV* pays lip service to the idea both in cautions in the descriptions of various disorders and by including an appendix that outlines how cultural factors might be described and a glossary of culture-bound syndromes (American Psychiatric Association, 1994, pp. 843–849). It seems unlikely that the information in this appendix would influence the procedures of most psychiatrists, since it remains so peripheral to their general worldview.

The Passage of Time

Maria Root (1992) is one of the very few who has pointed out that over time the effects of any specific trauma are obscured because of the effects of later events. She was speaking particularly about trauma. Many of the effects mentioned in earlier sections could also become obscured and disguised by other situations or events that happen between the original event and a diagnosis.

This factor needs to be considered more fully in the entire picture that makes up how we arrive at diagnoses. To date, we do not have enough information about the long-term effects of trauma and physical assaults and their interaction with other effects.

The Authority of the Examiner

It may be possible to assign to a person with a physical disease or other abnormality a diagnosis that would be more or less universally accepted—although we all know people who have received several different medical diagnoses for the same malady. It seems to happen most often when the disease is rare or exotic, although there are still areas where doctors disagree about whether a specific disease entity exists (i.e., chronic fatigue syndrome, various reactions to environmental toxins, etc.). It probably happens, although one hopes rarely, that a medical diagnosis is assigned because of the physician's attitudes toward the patient. One hears of physicians, for instance, who dismiss physical complaints by women, especially older women, as psychological and do not sufficiently study them further. We know, too, that a diagnosis of hysteria tends to mean that physicians do not look further for physical disorders (Leigh, Price, Ciarcia, & Mirassou, 1982).

The psychological/psychiatric realm is indefinite. Individual mental health practitioners decide on diagnoses according to their particular theoretical orientation, level and nature of training, and personal predilections. Although the official diagnostic manuals perch on their shelves, most practitioners use only a fraction of the possibilities available to them and have strong individualized preferences among the diagnostic categories. Hospitalized mental patients in the recent past usually were labeled schizophrenic, for example, more or less regardless of their individual symptomatology (Rosenhan, 1973). More recently, the bipolar mental illness diagnosis has achieved greater popularity among those who deal with the chronically mentally ill. The point remains the same, nevertheless. The degree of correspondence between the individual case and the diagnostic criteria is determined on an individual basis, case by case, without any external validation. Even the most rigorous studies in this area fail to find general agreement and cannot establish a large degree of reliability among examiners (Jampala, Sierles, & Taylor, 1988; Kirk & Kutchins, 1992). An earlier study by Temerlin (1968) found that the diagnostic setting and set given to the examiner had major effects upon whether a supposedly healthy individual received a psychiatric diagnosis, even one of psychosis. Langer and Abelson (1974) found that the same person was described as more disturbed when he was labeled a patient than when labeled a job applicant.

Guimon (1989) pointed out that:

> Psychiatric diagnosis is approached very differently according to whether the psychiatrist works within a biological, psychological, or social framework. Which frame he chooses depends on cognitive and affective factors, and even on religious and political beliefs; it is also conditioned by personality characteristics (e.g. authoritarianism, dogmatism and ability to tolerate frustration and ambiguity).
>
> Diagnostic bias, therefore, stems less from any technical limitations which are built into diagnostic and classificatory systems than from the mind and biases of the psychiatrist. (pp. 36–37)

For many years, the effects of gender, race, and social class on diagnosis (and treatment) have been debated. Although both sides have strong proponents, no actual scientific and/or professional consensus on the extent of such effects has as yet been reached. Research on these issues has actually declined in recent years, perhaps because of the touted view that the more precise definitions in *DSM-III* (and since) obviated the need to be concerned about the matter.

Kaplan, in response to critiques of her view that diagnostic criteria codify masculine-based assumptions about what behaviors are healthy and what behaviors are crazy (Kaplan, 1983a, p. 786), clarified her view that

> definitions of mental disorder and social deviance leave the rules for distinguishing between these two phenomena unclear; thus there is room for clinicians' values to play a role in making this distinction, and these values may reflect society's sexism. (Kaplan, 1983b, p. 802)

More recently, Pavkov, Lewis, and Lyons (1989) found that being black was a significant predictor of receiving a diagnosis of schizophrenia in Chicago hospitals. Dohrenwend (1990) has attempted to revive interest in the relationship between socioeconomic status and psychiatric disorders. Loring and Powell (1988) found that the sex and race of both client and psychiatrist influence diagnosis even when clear-cut diagnostic criteria are presented. They conclude that it would be premature to close the book on questions about the influence of sex and race on diagnosis.

Landrine (1992) studied the relationship of social stereotypes and psychiatric diagnosis among groups in a series of nine studies. She had previously identified what the literature stated about some of these relations. (In the following quotation, I have eliminated her considerable number of references):

> We know ... that lower-class people receive the diagnosis of schizophrenia far more often than any other status group; and, we know that lower-class blacks, minorities, and women have an exceptionally high probability of receiving that diagnosis. We also know that hysterical (histrionic) personality disorder diagnosis is almost exclusively attributed to unmarried women, and that the diagnosis of dependent personality is also attributed to women. We have known for decades that those who are diagnosed depressed are usually women, and that the women in question

are almost always married. We know that those diagnosed as ago-raphobics are almost always housewives, and that most other phobics also tend to be women. We know that most cases of multiple personality disorder tend to be women, or black men. On the other hand, we know that most drug abusers and alcoholics are men, and often minorities, as are the vast majority of paranoid personality disorders, narcissistic personality disorders, and compulsive personality disorders. Antisocial personalities, too, are almost always relatively young, lower-class (and frequently minority) men—men who outnumber women in any social class in that diagnostic category at a ratio of 10 to 1. Lastly, we know that these—and many other—epidemiological relationships have been stable for several generations, and we know that these patterns hold not only in the United States but also in other modern, industrialized, stratified societies—viz., in much of Europe and in Canada for example. (pp. xi–xii)

She suggested, however, that relating these findings to clinician bias represents an oversimplified view of the situation, because members of the groups mentioned often self-report the prototypical symptoms of the type of illness found in their groups. She suggests "that we *examine the political purposes served by, and the probable outcomes of any psychiatric taxonomy* (viz., behavioral, interpersonal, structural-family) in the context of *this* social order" [emphasis in original] (p. 185). She proposes that we place the various attributes back into the context of class exploitation, racial stratification, and patriarchy. She proposes structural and political rather than individual behavioral change to break down the system.

In the absence of sufficient evidence, I offer the diagram that follows as an illustration of the wide variety of elements that I see as potentially involved in the etiology of emotional and mental distress and pathology (see Figure 6.1). At this moment we do not know enough about the extent and degree to which any of them are involved in any particular case. It is eminently clear, however, that all of those listed under socioemotional factors as well as those that impose the values of society by means of the authority and judgment of the examiner have previously been insufficiently emphasized, explored, or perhaps even named. That applies as well to some of the factors listed as physical.

FIGURE 6.1. Factors in the Diagnosis of Psychopathology

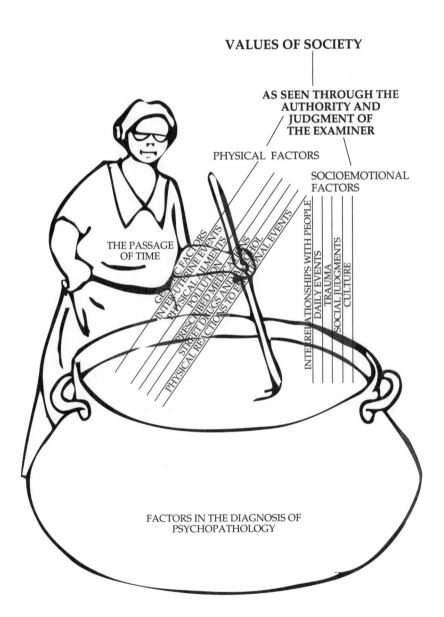

VALUES OF SOCIETY

AS SEEN THROUGH THE
AUTHORITY AND
JUDGMENT OF
THE EXAMINER

PHYSICAL FACTORS

SOCIOEMOTIONAL
FACTORS

THE PASSAGE
OF TIME

GENETIC FACTORS
INTRAUTERINE EVENTS
PHYSICAL AILMENTS
POLLUTION
PRESCRIBED MEDICATIONS
STREET DRUGS AND ALCOHOL
PHYSICAL REACTIONS TO EMOTIONAL EVENTS

INTERRELATIONSHIPS WITH PEOPLE
DAILY EVENTS
TRAUMA
SOCIAL JUDGMENTS
CULTURE

FACTORS IN THE DIAGNOSIS OF
PSYCHOPATHOLOGY

CHAPTER 7

Breaking Out
of the Pigeonholes:
Feminist Approaches

THE FEMINIST REACTION TO DIAGNOSIS OVER TIME

FROM THE START of the most recent feminist movement until the preparations for the publication of *DSM-III-R* in 1987, there was a great deal of activity and interest within the mental health professions in women's issues. This has included research specifically with and about women as well as reexamination of psychological theories in use to see if they addressed women's concerns. Usually, the finding was that they did not. Female clinicians studied Freudian and other theories and attempted to modify them so that they were more inclusive of women's issues (see Sturdivant, 1980, for an account of the early history of feminist therapy). Very little of this literature or the ideas behind it have influenced the *DSM*s. Feminist therapy was, however, included as one possible intervention for the social work Person-In-Environment (PIE) system (Karls & Wandrei, 1994b).

Although the study of female psychology had begun and has flourished up until the present, feminist psychology generally ignored the issues specific to formal diagnosis before the debate surrounding *DSM-III-R*. Since feminist therapists generally dealt one on one (or in small groups) with client women outside of hospitals and clinics, they were not often directly confronted with the political and social issues that surround diagnosis. Occasionally,

151

someone would raise some issues involving hospitalized or chronically mentally ill women—but in general diagnosis was not a major focus of concern.

The controversy over *DSM-III-R* changed that. Informally, feminist therapists have even thanked Robert Spitzer (admittedly with irony) for awakening them to the important issues psychodiagnosis raises. Among these are, of course, stigmatization and use of the systems in stereotyped and dehumanizing ways.

In the years since then, for reasons in addition to raised consciousness, diagnosis has slowly grown in importance for feminist clinicians. As alternative facilities like battered women's shelters and rape trauma clinics have become more institutionalized and have received grant money from private and public sources, they have had to account to these outside sources, often in terms of client diagnoses using the *DSM*. At the private level, psychotherapy used to be commonly provided on an independent fee-for-service basis, but centralized health maintenance organizations, which also require diagnoses, are gradually changing that, forcing practitioners to use the only available system, the *DSM*s. Along the way, however, we have begun both to analyze the system from a feminist perspective and to explore alternatives.

As Laura Brown (1988) indicated (see chapter 1, p. 3), diagnostic thinking has always been and needs to continue to be an important aspect of feminist clinical work. Attempts are being made, within feminist circles at least, to put what we have been learning to use.

SOME DEVELOPING FEMINIST APPROACHES

Feminist clinicians relied heavily on the PTSD diagnosis after *DSM-III* was published in 1980. It enabled us to identify and make sense of the distress our clients presented to us without having to pathologize the women themselves, since it was (and is) the only major diagnosis that could be used for "normal" people reacting normally to abnormal circumstances. The relationship between chronic abuse, both personal and cultural, and the development of personality as it is supposedly exemplified in the axis II diagnoses is finally being explored and studied. Many feminists, among them Herman (1992a, 1992b), have discussed the problems raised by diagnosing with these labels.

Trying to work within the *DSM* framework, Lenore Walker (1986) first suggested a category of disorders she envisioned as somewhere between the axis II personality disorders and the PTSD diagnosis. She suggested a category of abuse disorders, which she saw as more pervasive than PTSD but connected less to what could be called core personality than the personality disorders are. She tentatively suggested that persons with these situationally derived disorders

> could be seen to have disturbances in the nature of the reinforce-ment (i.e., blunted affect, dissociation so as not to feel pain, dis-turbance in sexual pleasure, etc.); in the reinforcement source (i.e., self-mutilation, uncontrollable sexual abuse from father, love from father, uncontrollable physical abuse from husband, love from husband, abuse of others) and different instrumental styles such as passive, active, or mixed types which could produce pas-sivity in some battered women, aggression in abusive mates, or aggression in battered women who abuse their children or abu-sive partners. (p. 17)

She suggested that pervasive and enduring symptoms would be apparent as long as the individual faced the threat of potential dan-ger (Walker, 1987).

Laura Brown (1987) took these ideas even further. She suggested a category of oppression artifact disorders, which she thinks is needed to

> take into account the life-time learning experiences of living in a sexist, racist, homophobic, ageist, and otherwise oppressive cul-tural context. Most individuals who are not securely ensconced within a culturally valued group (e.g., white, upper-middle class heterosexual able-bodied young males) will have repeated expo-sure throughout their lifetime to the overt expressions of such oppression. Depending on the particular context, the penalties for failure to respond correctly can vary from annoying (being verbally harassed on the street for simply being female) to life-threatening (being raped for simply being female). Women, peo-ple of color, sexual minorities, disabled people, and elders all may experience a social and interpersonal context of forced choice in which the adoption of certain patterns of response, and certain perceptions of self allow for an easier fit with an oppres-sive society. (pp. 12–13)

These provocative ideas are just the first step, however. Both Walker's and Brown's proposals represent attempts to work within the current *DSM-IV* framework. The reasons for trying to do so should be obvious at this point. In some fashion, we have to deal with the world around us, which accepts the *DSM*. Making some change in it, if we can, is one viable strategy.

OPEN QUESTIONS

I have described the mental image I have of the etiology of emotional and mental disorders as a stewpot or cauldron. The myriad ingredients are poured in and stirred together over time so that no single ingredient is readily identifiable. However, since there is much about the separate ingredients of the stew that we cannot identify with certainty, we would have to learn much more than we presently know before such a detailed schema based on etiology could be used. We need, for example, to learn about physical causation. Similarly, psychoanalytic thinking blinded us for a long time to the possibilities of any external causes for internal ills. We have been moving away from that kind of thinking and must remain open to the possibilities of all manner of stimulating factors.

As I have suggested, the extent to which trauma in its broadest sense (which, to my mind, would encompass the effects of oppression as described by Laura Brown) is an important cause of emotional distress has not been significantly acknowledged. It is increasingly difficult for me to see PTSD as separate and distinct from all other pathologies and psychological difficulties. The growing literature on the proportions of psychiatric patients of various types who have been physically and sexually abused makes that clear (Carmen, Reiker, & Mills, 1984; Jacobson & Richardson, 1987; Rosenfeld, 1979; Russell, 1986). With this in mind, we have to question other assumptions about the manuals since *DSM-III*, most particularly those related to the axis II personality disorder diagnoses (Brown, 1987). The recent evidence strongly suggests that many people who have been diagnosed with borderline personality disorders (Barnard & Hirsch, 1985; Gross, Doerr, Caldirola, Guzinski, & Ripley, 1980; Herman & van der Kolk, 1987) or even multiple personality disorders (Coons & Milstein, 1984; Herman & van der Kolk, 1987; Putnam, Guroff, Silberman, Barban, & Post, 1986; Saltman & Solomon, 1982) can be better treated if they are seen as long-term chronic PTSD sufferers, since many of them have indeed suffered through long periods of physical and/or sexual abuse in addition to other forms of psychological abuse.

I sometimes think of myself as seeing the many changes in society differently through each of my two eyes. With one, I see how far we have come. With the other, I see how far we yet have to go. As I write, for example, I find myself thinking about a young hospitalized woman I have seen who, while she has some delusional ideas, seems to have been hospitalized by her family mainly to prevent her from getting pregnant and having another child beyond the four she already has had. It was easier to hospitalize her than to shake her conditioning that she must do whatever a man wants her to do—including, incidentally, a man on the hospital's cleaning staff. I suppose we can call it progress that she has not been involuntarily sterilized! It is not progress that the alternative is medication and hospitalization. To my mind, the dilemma about how we deal with women like her, the extent to which her actual *DSM* diagnosis and treatment is irrelevant, typifies the problems we have to face.

It is clear that the official framework through which society views emotional ailments and distress does not adequately deal with our concerns. We have to continue our work both inside and outside that framework. Like it or not, it is so pervasive that we must use it at times whether we wish to or not. At the same time, we cannot stop working on our own, formulating and systematizing our own ideas, agitating to get them included, and influencing those outside our framework who maintain such power over so many women's lives.

It was only while researching and writing this book that I encountered the alternative systems I have described. That I, who considers myself someone who tries to keep up with trends in the field, did not know about them tells me that the few alternatives out there are invisible to most practitioners. The *DSM*s direct our thinking into certain well-traveled paths that have become ruts that are hard to escape. We have to follow them in many clinical circumstances, but that does not mean we should stop working hard to forge new routes.

I have been particularly impressed by the PIE system devised by the social work profession. Their way around the dilemma presented by the prominence of the *DSM*s was to include the psychiatric diagnoses—but in a way that makes it possible for them to effectively ignore it.

In 1986, I formulated a set of criteria for developing a feminist theory of personality (Lerman, 1986). Many feminists have indicated that my ideas have proved useful to them. One of the criteria I mentioned was "remaining close to the data of experience"

(p. 176). This concept seems especially meaningful in dealing with the dilemmas provoked by diagnostic issues. I find the PIE system to be most in accord with what I was trying to describe and at this time recommend that other feminist therapists acquaint themselves with it so that we can more fully explore its potential.

REFERENCES

Alagna, Sheryle A., & Hamilton, Jean A. (1986). *Science in the service of mythology: The psychopathologizing of menstruation.* Paper presented at the Convention of the American Psychological Association, Washington, DC.

American Psychiatric Association. (1952). *Diagnostic and statistic manual of mental disorders.* Washington, DC: Author.

American Psychiatric Association. (1968). *Diagnostic and statistical manual of mental disorders* (2nd ed.). Washington, DC: Author.

American Psychiatric Association. (1974). *Diagnostic and statistical manual of mental disorders* (2nd ed., 7th printing). Washington, DC: Author.

American Psychiatric Association. (1980). *Diagnostic and statistical manual of mental disorders* (3rd ed.). Washington, DC: Author.

American Psychiatric Association. (1987). *Diagnostic and statistical manual of mental disorders* (3rd ed., rev.). Washington, DC: Author.

American Psychiatric Association. (1991). *DSM-IV options book: Work in Progress (9/1/91).* Washington, DC: American Psychiatric Association Task Force on *DSM-IV.*

American Psychiatric Association. (1993). *DSM-IV Draft Criteria: 3/1/93.* Washington, DC: American Psychiatric Association Task Force on *DSM-IV.*

American Psychiatric Association. (1994). *Diagnostic and statistical manual of mental disorders* (4th ed.). Washington, DC: Author.

Andrews, Bernice, Valentine, Elizabeth R., & Valentine, John D. (1995). Depression and eating disorders following abuse in childhood in two generations of women. *British Journal of Clinical Psychology, 34,* 37–52.

Atchison, M., & McFarlane, A. C. (1994). A review of dissociation and dissociative disorders. *Australian and New Zealand Journal of Psychiatry, 28,* 591–599.

Barnard, Charles P., & Hirsch, Cynthia. (1985). Borderline personality and victims of incest. *Psychological Reports, 57,* 715–718.

Barton, Walter E. (1987). *The history and influence of the American Psychiatric Association.* Washington, DC: American Psychiatric Press.

Bateson, Gregory, Jackson, Don D., Haley, Jay, & Weakland, J. (1956). Toward a theory of schizophrenia. *Behavioral Science, 1,* 251–264.

Bayer, Ronald. (1981). *Homosexuality and American psychiatry.* New York: Basic Books.

Bayer, Ronald, & Spitzer, Robert L. (1985). Neurosis, psychodynamics, and DSM-III. *Archives of General Psychiatry, 42,* 187–196.

Beitchman, Joseph H., Zucker, Kenneth J., Hood, Jane E., DaCosta, Granville A., Akman, Donna, & Cassavia, Erika. (1992). A review of the long-term effects of child sexual abuse. *Child Abuse and Neglect, 16,* 101–118.

Benjamin, Lorna Smith. (1974). Structural analysis of social behavior. *Psychological Review, 81,* 392–425.

Benjamin, Lorna Smith. (1994). The bridge is supposed to reach the clinic, not just another corner of the academy. *Psychological Inquiry, 5,* 336–343.

Benjamin, Lorna Smith, & Wonderlich, Stephen A. (1994). Social perceptions and borderline personality disorder: The relation to mood disorders. *Journal of Abnormal Psychology, 103,* 610–624.

Berger, David M. (1971). Hysteria: In search of the animus. *Comprehensive Psychiatry, 12*(3), 277–286.

Bettelheim, Bruno. (1969). Student revolt: The hard core. *Vital Speeches of the Day, 35,* 405–410.

Binitie, Ayo. (1988). Diagnosis and classification of mental disorders and alcohol- and drug-related problems in Nigeria. In Juan E. Mezzich & Michael von Cranach (Eds.), *International classification in psychiatry: Unity and diversity* (pp. 65–72). New York: Cambridge University Press.

Blashfield, Roger K. (1984). *The classification of psychopathology: Neo-Kraepelinian and quantitative approaches.* New York: Plenum Press.

Blashfield, Roger K., & Breen, Mark S. (1989). Face validity of the DSM-III-R personality disorders. *American Journal of Psychiatry, 146,* 1575–1579.

Blashfield, Roger K., & Draguns, Juris G. (1976a). Evaluative criteria for psychiatric classification. *Journal of Abnormal Psychology, 85*(2), 140–150.

Blashfield, Roger K., & Draguns, Juris G. (1976b). Toward a taxonomy of psychopathology: The purpose of psychiatric classification. *British Journal of Psychiatry, 129,* 574–583.

Blashfield, Roger K., & Livesley, W. John. (1991). Metaphorical analysis of psychiatric classification as a psychological test. *Journal of Abnormal Psychology, 100*(3), 262–270.

Blum, Jeffrey D. (1978). On changes in psychiatric diagnosis over time. *American Psychologist, 33,* 1017–1031.

Bornstein, Robert F. (1996). Sex differences in dependent personality disorder prevalence rates. *Clinical Psychology: Science and Practice, 3,* 1–12.

Boulding, Elise. (1992a). *The underside of history* (Vol. I). Newbury Park, CA: Sage Publications.

Boulding, Elise. (1992b). *The underside of history* (Vol. II). Newbury Park, CA: Sage Publications.

Boyd, Jeffrey H., Burke, Jack D. Jr., Gruenberg, Ernest, Holzer, Charles E. III, Rae, Donald S., George, Linda K., Karno, Marvin, Stoltzman, Roger, McEvoy, Larry, & Nestadt, Gerald. (1984). Exclusion criteria of DSM-III. *Archives of General Psychiatry, 41,* 983–989.

Boyle, Mary. (1990). Is schizophrenia what it was? A re-analysis of Kraepelin's and Bleuler's population. *Journal of the History of the Behavioral Sciences, 26,* 323–333.

Breggin, Peter R. (1990). Brain damage, dementia and persistent cognitive-dysfunction associated with neuroleptic drugs: Evidence, etiology, implications. *Journal of Mind and Behavior, 11,* 425–464.

Breggin, Peter R. (1991). *Toxic psychiatry.* New York: St. Martin's Press.

Breslau, Naomi, & Davis, Glenn C. (1987). Posttraumatic stress disorder: The stressor criterion. *Journal of Nervous and Mental Disease, 175*(5), 255–264.

Briere, John. (1995). Science versus politics in the delayed memory debate: A commentary. *The Counseling Psychologist, 23*(2), 290–293.

Brill, Henry. (1972). Classification in psychiatry. In Alfred M. Freedman & Harold I. Kaplan (Eds.), *Diagnosing mental illness: Evaluation in psychiatry and psychology* (pp. 182–189). New York: Atheneum.

Broverman, Inge K., Broverman, David M., Clarkson, Frank E., Rosencrantz, Philip, & Vogel, S. (1970). Sex role stereotypes and clinical judgment of mental health. *Journal of Consulting and Clinical Psychology, 34,* 1–7.

Brown, Laura S. (1984). Finding new language: Getting beyond analytic verbal shorthand in feminist therapy. *Women and Therapy, 3*(1), 73–80.

Brown, Laura. (1987, August). *Towards a new conceptual paradigm for the Axis II diagnoses.* Paper presented at the Convention of the American Psychological Association, New York.

Brown, Laura S. (1988). *Feminist therapy perspectives on psychodiagnosis: Beyond the DSM and ICD.* Paper presented to the International Congress on Mental Health Care for Women, Amsterdam, The Netherlands.

Brown, Laura S. (1994). *Subversive dialogues: Theory in feminist therapy.* New York: Basic Books.

Brown, Laura S. (1995). Toward not forgetting: The science and politics of memory. *The Counseling Psychologist, 23*(2), 310–314.

Brown, Phil. (1987). Diagnostic conflict and contradiction in psychiatry. *Journal of Health and Social Behavior, 28,* 37–50.

Brown, Phil. (1990). The name game: Toward a sociology of diagnosis. *Journal of Mind and Behavior, 11,* 385–406.

Browne, Angela. (1987). *When battered women kill.* New York: Free Press.

Bryer, Jeffrey B., Nelson, Bernadette A., Miller, Jean Baker, & Krol, Pamela A. (1987). Childhood sexual and physical abuse as factors in adult psychiatric illness. *American Journal of Psychiatry, 144,* 1426–1430.

Bullough, Vern, & Voght, Martha. (1973). Women, menstruation and nineteenth-century medicine. *Bulletin of the History of Medicine, 47,* 66–82.

Burstein, Allan. (1985). Posttraumatic stress disorder. *Journal of Clinical Psychiatry, 46,* 300–301.

Cafferata, Gail Lee, Kasper, Judith, & Bernstein, Amy. (1983). Family roles, structure and stressors in relation to sex differences in obtaining psychotropic drugs. *Journal of Health and Social Behavior, 24,* 132–143.

Campbell, Robert J. (1989). *Psychiatric dictionary* (6th ed.). New York: Oxford University Press.

Caplan, Paula J. (1987). The psychiatric association's failure to meet its own standards: The dangers of self-defeating personality disorder as a category. *Journal of Personality Disorders, 2,* 178–182.

Caplan, Paula J. (1991). How *do* they decide who is normal? The bizarre, but true, tale of the *DSM* process. *Canadian Psychology/Psychologie canadienne, 32,* 162–170.

Carlin, Albert S., Kemper, Kathi, Ward, Nicholas G., Sowell, Heather, Gustafson, Belinda, & Stevens, Nancy. (1994). The effects of differences in objective and subjective definitions of childhood physical abuse on estimates of its incidence and relationship to psychopathology. *Child Abuse and Neglect, 18*(5), 393–399.

Carmen, Elaine (Hilberman). (1985). Masochistic personality disorder DSM-III-R: Critique. Unpublished paper.

Carmen, Elaine (Hilberman), Reiker, Patricia Perri, & Mills, Trudy. (1984). Victims of violence and psychiatric illness. *American Journal of Psychiatry, 14,* 378–383.

Carson, Robert C. (1991). Dilemmas in the pathway of the DSM-IV. *Journal of Abnormal Psychology, 100*(3), 302–307.

Cash, Thomas E., & Henry, Patricia E. (1995). Women's body images: The results of a national survey in the U.S.A. *Sex Roles, 33,* 19–28.

Cattell, Raymond B. (1983). Let's end the duel. *American Psychologist, 38,* 769–776.

Chodoff, Paul. (1982). Hysteria and women. *American Journal of Psychiatry, 139,* 545–551.

Clark, L. A., Watson, D., & Reynolds, S. (1995). Diagnosis and classification of psychopathology: Challenges to the current system and future directions. *Annual Review of Psychology, 46,* 121–153.

Cohen, David. (1994). Neuroleptic drug treatment of schizophrenia: The state of the confusion. *Journal of Mind and Behavior, 15,* 139–156.

Cohen, Sheldon, & Rodriguez, Mario S. (1995). Pathways linking affective disturbances and physical disorders. *Health Psychology, 14*(5), 374–380.

Coons, Philip M., & Milstein, Victor. (1984). Rape and post-traumatic stress in multiple personality. *Psychological Reports, 55,* 839–845.

Cooper, John E. (1988). The presentation of psychiatric classification. In Juan E. Mezzich & Michael von Cranach (Eds.), *International classification in psychiatry: Unity and diversity* (pp. 322–331). New York: Cambridge University Press.

Cooper, John, & Sartorius, Norman. (1977). Cultural and temporal variations in schizophrenia: A speculation on the importance of industrialization. *British Journal of Psychiatry, 130,* 50–55.

Committee on Women of the American Psychiatric Association (1985, September 21). Premenstrual Dysphoric Disorder—Facts and Issues.

Courtois, Christine A. (1995). Scientist-practitioners and the delayed memory controversy: Scientific standards and the need for collaboration. *The Counseling Psychologist, 23*(2), 294–299.

Cutler, Susan E., & Nolen-Hoeksema, Susan. (1991). Accounting for sex differences through female victimization: Childhood sexual abuse. *Sex Roles, 24*(7/8), 425–438.

Darves-Bornoz, J. M., Lemperiere, T., Degiovanni, A., & Gaillard, P. (1995). Sexual victimization in women with schizophrenia and bipolar disorder. *Social Psychiatry and Psychiatric Epidemiology, 30,* 78–84.

Davidson, Jonathan R. T., & Foa, Edna B. (1991). Diagnostic issues in posttraumatic stress disorder: Considerations for the DSM-IV. *Journal of Abnormal Psychology, 100*(3), 346–355.

Deutsch, K. W. (1966). On theories, taxonomies and models as communication codes for organizing information. *Behavioural Science, 11,* 1–17.

Dick, C. L., Bland, R. C., & Newman, S. C. (1994). Panic disorder. *Acta Psychiatrica Scandanivica,* (Suppl. 376), 45–53.

Digman, John M. (1994). Historical antecedents of the five-factor model. In Costa, Paul T. Jr., & Widiger, Thomas A. (Eds.), *Personality disorders and the five-factor model of personality* (pp. 13–18). Washington, DC: American Psychological Association.

Dohrenwend, Bruce P. (1990). Socioeconomic status (SES) and psychiatric disorders: Are the issues still compelling? *Social Psychiatry and Psychiatric Epidemiology, 25,* 41–47.

Dorland's Illustrated Medical Dictionary, 24th ed. (1965). Philadelphia: W. B. Saunders.

Downing, Charles J. (1983). A behavior classification system for counselors: A new look at psychopathology. *Humanistic Education and Development 21*(4), 138–145.

Edelstein, Ludwig. (1943). The Hippocratic oath: Text, translation and interpretation. *Bulletin of the History of Medicine* (Suppl. 1), 3.

Eisenbruch, Maurice. (1992). Toward a culturally sensitive DSM: Cultural bereavement in Cambodian refugees and the traditional healer as taxonomist. *Journal of Nervous and Mental Disease, 180,* 8–10.

Ellard, John. (1987). Did schizophrenia exist before the eighteenth century? *Australian and New Zealand Journal of Psychiatry, 21,* 306–314.

Enns, Carolyn Zerbe, McNeilly, Cheryl L., Corkery, Julie Madison, & Gilbert, Mary S. (1995). The debate about delayed memories of child sexual abuse: A feminist perspective. *The Counseling Psychologist, 23*(2), 181–279.

Everill, Joanne T., & Waller, Glenn. (1995). Reported sexual abuse and eating psychopathology: A review of the evidence for a causal link. *International Journal of Eating Disorders, 18*(1), 1–11.

Farber, Seth. (1990). Institutional mental health and social control: The ravages of epistemological hubris. *Journal of Mind and Behavior, 11,* 285–299.

Faust, David, & Miner, Richard A. (1986). The empiricist and his new clothes: DSM-III in perspective. *American Journal of Psychiatry, 143,* 962–967.

Feighner, John P., Robins, Eli, Guze, Samuel B., Woodruff, Robert A. Jr., Winokur, George, & Muñoz, Rodrigo. (1972). Diagnostic criteria for use in psychiatric research. *Archives of General Psychiatry, 26,* 57–62.

Fidell, Linda S. (1980). Sex role stereotypes and the American physician. *Psychology of Women Quarterly, 4*(3), 313–330.

Fidell, Linda S. (1981). Sex differences in psychotropic drug use. *Professional Psychology, 12*(1), 156–162.

Finkelhor, David, Hotaling, Gerald, Lewis, I. A., & Smith, Christine. (1990). Sexual abuse in a national survey of adult men and women: Prevalence, characteristics, and risk factors. *Child Abuse and Neglect, 14,* 19–28.

Foder, Iris E. (1996). A woman and her body: The cycles of pride and shame. In Robert G. Lee & Gordon Wheeler (Eds.), *The voice of shame: Silence and connection in psychotherapy.* San Francisco: Jossey-Bass.

Fogarty, F., Russell, J. M., Newman, S. C., & Bland, R. C. (1994). Mania. *Acta Psychiatrica Scandinavica* (Suppl. 376), 16–23.

Foulds, Graham A. (1976). *The hierarchical nature of personal illness.* London: Academic Press.

Frances, Allen, & Widiger, Thomas A. (1986). Methodological issues in personality disorder diagnosis. In Theodore Millon & Gerald L. Klerman (Eds.), *Contemporary directions in psychopathology: Toward the DSM-IV* (pp. 381–402). New York: Guilford.

Frank, Robert T. (1931). The hormonal causes of premenstrual tension. *Archives of Neurology and Psychiatry, 26,* 1053–1057.

Freud, Sigmund. (1962). The aetiology of hysteria. In James Strachey (Ed. and Trans.), *The standard edition of the complete psychological works of Sigmund Freud* (Vol. 3, pp. 191–221). London: Hogarth Press. (Original work published 1896)

Freud, Sigmund. (1961). The dissolution of the Oedipus complex. In James Strachey (Ed. and Trans.), *The standard edition of the complete psychological works of Sigmund Freud* (Vol. 19, pp. 173–179). London: Hogarth Press. (Original work published 1924)

Gilman, Charlotte Perkins. (1973). *The yellow wallpaper.* Old Westbury, N.Y.: The Feminist Press. (Original work published 1899)

Gilman, Charlotte Perkins. (1915). Dr. Clair's place. *The Forerunner,* 6(6), 141–145.

Gitlin, Michael J., & Pasnau, Robert O. (1989). Psychiatric syndromes linked to reproductive function in women: A review of current knowledge. *American Journal of Psychiatry, 146,* 1413–1422.

Golding, Jacqueline M. (1996). Sexual assault history and women's reproductive and sexual health. *Psychology of Women Quarterly,* 20, 101–121.

Goldman, Arnold R., Bohr, Ronald H., & Steinberg, Thomas A. (1973). On posing as mental patients: Reminiscences and recommendations. In Richard H. Price & Bruce Denner (Eds.), *The making of a mental patient* (pp. 186–197). New York: Holt, Rinehart and Winston.

Gonsiorek, John C. (Ed.). (1995). *Breach of trust: Sexual exploitation by health care professionals and clergy.* Thousand Oaks, CA: Sage Publications.

Gove, Walter R. (1980). Mental illness and psychiatric treatment among women. *Psychology of Women Quarterly,* 4(3), 345–362.

Green, Bonnie L., Lindy, Jacob D., & Grace, Marcy C. (1985). Post-traumatic stress disorder: Toward DSM-IV. *Journal of Nervous and Mental Disease, 173*(7), 406–411.

Greenwald, Deborah. (1992). Psychotic disorders with emphasis on schizophrenia. In Laura S. Brown & Mary Ballou (Eds.), *Personality and psychopathology: Feminist reappraisals* (pp. 144–176). New York: Guilford.

Grob, Gerald N. (1991). Origins of DSM-I: A study in appearance and reality. *American Journal of Psychiatry, 148*(4), 421–431.

Gross, Robert J., Doerr, Hans, Caldirola, Della, Guzinski, Gay M., & Ripley, Herbert S. (1980). Borderline syndrome and incest in chronic pelvic pain patients. *International Journal of Psychiatry in Medicine, 10*(1), 79–96.

Guimon, José. (1989). The biases of psychiatric diagnosis. *British Journal of Psychiatry, 154*(Suppl. 4), 33–37.

Haghighat, Rahman. (1994). Cultural sensitivity: ICD-10 versus DSM-III-R. *International Journal of Social Psychiatry, 40*(3), 189–193.

Hall, Richard C. W., Popkin, Michael K., Devaul, Richard A., Faillace, Louis A., & Stickney, Sondra K. (1978). Physical illness presenting as psychiatric disease. *Archives of General Psychiatry, 35,* 1315–1320.

Hamilton, Jean. (Fall 1987/Spring 1988). Is media coverage on the diagnostic controversy an index of history in-the-making for women in science? *Coalition Report: Newsletter of the National Coalition for Women's Mental Health*, 9–11.

Hamilton, Jean A. (1989). Emotional consequences of victimization and discrimination in "special populations" of women. *Psychiatric Clinics of North America, 12*(1), 35–51.

Hamilton, Jean A., & Gallant, Sheryle J. (Alagna). (1988). On a premenstrual psychiatric diagnosis: What's in a name? *Professional Psychology: Research and Practice, 19,* 271–278.

Hamilton, Jean A., & Jensvold, Margaret. (1992). Personality, psychopathology, and depressions in women. In Laura S. Brown & Mary Ballou (Eds.), *Personality and psychopathology: Feminist reappraisals* (pp. 116–143). New York: Guilford.

Hamilton, Sandra, Rothbart, Myron, & Dawes, Robyn M. (1986). Sex bias, diagnosis and DSM-III. *Sex Roles, 15*(5/6), 269–274.

Helmchen, H. (1983). Multiaxial classification in psychiatry. *Comprehensive Psychiatry, 24,* 20–24.

Helzer, John E., & Coryell, William. (1983). More on the DSM III: How consistent are precise criteria? *Biological Psychiatry, 18,* 1201–1203.

Herman, Judith Lewis. (1992a). Complex PTSD: A syndrome in survivors of prolonged and repeated trauma. *Journal of Traumatic Stress, 5,* 377–391.

Herman, Judith Lewis. (1992b). *Trauma and recovery: The aftermath of violence—from domestic abuse to political terror.* New York: Basic Books.

Herman, Judith L., & van der Kolk, Bessel A. (1987). Traumatic antecedents of borderline personality disorder. In Bessel A. van der Kolk (Ed.), *Psychological trauma* (pp. 111–126). Washington, DC: American Psychiatric Press.

Hoch, Paul, & Polatin, Philip. (1949). Pseudoneurotic forms of schizophrenia. *Psychiatric Quarterly, 23,* 248–276.

Hoffman, Robert S. (1982, August 27). Diagnostic errors in the evaluation of behavioral disorders. *Journal of the American Medical Association, 248*(8), 964–967.

Jacobi, Mary Putnam. (1978). *The question of rest for women during menstruation.* Farmingdale, NY: Dabor Social Science Publications. (Original work published 1886)

Jacobi, Mary Putnam. (1885). Theories of menstruation—new theory. Studies in endometritis. *American Journal of Obstetrics, 18,* 376–386.

Jacobi, Mary Putnam. (1890). Female physicians for insane women. *Medical Record, 37,* 543–544.

Jacobi, Mary Putnam. (1925). Modern female invalidism. In *Mary Putnam Jacobi: A pathfinder in medicine* edited by the Women's Medical Association of New York City (pp. 478–482). New York: G. P. Putnam's Sons. (Originally written in 1895)

Jacobs, David H. (1994). Environmental failure—oppression is the only cause of psychopathology. *Journal of Mind and Behavior, 15,* 1–8.

Jacobson, Andrea, & Richardson, Bonnie. (1987). Assault experiences of 100 psychiatric inpatients: Evidence of the need for routine inquiry. *American Journal of Psychiatry, 144*(7), 908–913.

JAMA 100 years ago: Castration in nervous and mental diseases. (1986, November 21). *Journal of the American Medical Association, 256,* 2680.

Jampala, V. Chowdary, Sierles, Frederick S., & Taylor, Michael Alan. (1988). The use of the DSM-III in the United States: A case of not going by the book. *Comprehensive Psychiatry, 29,* 39–47.

Johnson, Marilyn. (1980). Mental illness and psychiatric treatment among women: A response. *Psychology of Women Quarterly, 4*(3), 363–371.

Kagan, Jerome. (1984). *The nature of the child.* New York: Basic Books.

Kaplan, Marcie. (1983a). A woman's view of DSM-III. *American Psychologist, 38,* 786–792.

Kaplan, Marcie. (1983b). The issues in sex bias in DSM-III: Comments on the articles by Spitzer, Williams and Kass. *American Psychologist, 38,* 802–803.

Kardiner, Abraham. (1941). *The traumatic neuroses of war.* New York: P. Hoeber.

Karls, James M., & Wandrei, Karin E. (1992). PIE: A new language for social work. *Social Work, 37*(1), 80–85.

Karls, James M., & Wandrei, Karin E. (1994a). PIE: A system for describing and classifying problems of social functioning. In James M. Karls & Karin E. Wandrei (Eds.), *Person-In-Environment system: The PIE classification system for social functioning problems* (pp. 3–21). Washington, DC: NASW Press.

Karls, James M., & Wandrei, Karin E. (1994b). *PIE manual: Person-in-environment system.* Washington, DC: NASW Press.

Kaschak, Ellyn. (1992). *Engendered lives: A new psychology of women's experience.* New York: Basic Books.

Kaslow, Florence W. (Ed.). (1996). *Handbook of relational diagnosis and dysfunctional family patterns.* New York: John Wiley & Sons.

Kass, Frederic, Spitzer, Robert L., & Williams, Janet B. W. (1983). An empirical study of the issue of sex bias in the diagnostic criteria of DSM-III axis II personality disorders. *American Psychologist, 38,* 799–801.

Kass, Frederic, Spitzer, Robert L., Williams, Janet B. W., & Widiger, Thomas. (1989). Self-defeating personality disorder and DSM-III-R: Development of the diagnostic criteria. *American Journal of Psychiatry, 146,* 1022–1026.

Kendell, Robert E. (1988). Priorities for the next decade. In Juan E. Mezzich & Michael von Cranach (Eds.), *International classification in psychiatry: Unity and diversity* (pp. 332–340). New York: Cambridge University Press.

Kessler, Ronald C., McGonagle, Katherine A., Zhao, Shanyang, Nelson, Christopher B., Hughes, Michael, Eshleman, Suzann, Wittchen, Hans-Ulrich, & Kendler, Kenneth S. (1994). Lifetime and 12-month prevalence of DSM-III-R psychiatric disorders in the United States: Results from the national comorbidity survey. *Archives of General Psychiatry, 51*(1), 8–19.

Kety, Seymour S. (1975). Classification in science. In Theodore Blau, Mortimer Brown, Arthur Centor, Martin M. Katz, Maurice Lorr, & J. R. Newbrough (Eds.), *Report of the Ad hoc Task Force on Behavioral Classification. I Classification: The State of the Science; II The State of the Art in Application* (pp. 8–14). Washington, DC: American Psychological Association.

Keye, William R. Jr. (Ed.). (1988). *The premenstrual syndrome.* Philadelphia: W. B. Saunders.

Keyser, Lucy. (1986, May 26). Sexist definitions of mental illness? *Insight,* 20–21.

King, Charles R. (1989). Parallels between neurasthenia and premenstrual syndrome. *Women and Health, 15*(4), 1–23.

Kirk, Stuart A., & Kutchins, Herb. (1988). Deliberate misdiagnosis in mental health practice. *Social Service Review,* 225–237.

Kirk, Stuart A., & Kutchins, Herb. (1992). *The selling of DSM: The rhetoric of science in psychiatry.* New York: Aldine de Gruyter.

Kirk, Stuart A., & Kutchins, Herb. (1995). How scientific is the DSM-IV? Paper presented at the American Psychological Association Convention, New York City.

Klerman, Gerald L. (1986). Historical perspectives on contemporary schools of psychopathology. In Theodore Millon & Gerald L. Klerman (Eds.), *Contemporary directions in psychopathology: Toward the DSM-IV* (pp. 3–28). New York: Guilford.

Klonoff, Elizabeth A., & Landrine, Hope. (1995). The schedule of sexist events. A Measure of lifetime and recent sexist discrimination in women's lives. *Psychology of Women Quarterly, 19,* 439–472.

Klonoff, Elizabeth A., & Landrine, Hope. (in press). *Preventing misdiagnosis of women: A guide to physical disorders with psychiatric symptoms.* Newbury Park, CA: Sage Publications.

Knopf, William F. (1970). A history of the concept of neurosis, with a memoir of William Cullen. *American Journal of Psychiatry, 127*(1), 120–124.

Kramer, Morton. (1988). Historical roots and structural bases of the International Classification of Diseases. In Juan E. Mezzich & Michael von Cranach (Eds.), *International classification in psychiatry: Unity and diversity* (pp. 3–29). New York: Cambridge University Press.

Kritek, Phyllis B. (1985). Nursing diagnosis in perspective: Response to a critique. *Image: The Journal of Nursing Scholarship, 17*(1), 3–8.

Kroll, Jerome. (1979). Philosophical foundations of French and U.S. nosology. *American Journal of Psychiatry, 136*(9), 1135–1138.

Landrine, Hope. (1988). Revising the framework of abnormal psychology. In Phyllis Bronstein & Kathryn Quina (Eds.), *Teaching a psychology of people: Resources for gender and sociocultural awareness* (pp. 37–44). Washington, DC: American Psychological Association.

Landrine, Hope. (1992). *The politics of madness.* New York: Peter Lang.

Landrine, Hope, Klonoff, Elizabeth A., Gibbs, Jeannine, Manning, Vickie, & Lund, Marlene. (1995). Physical and psychiatric correlates of gender discrimination; An application of the Schedule of Sexist Events. *Psychology of Women Quarterly, 19,* 473–492.

Langer, Ellen J., & Abelson, Robert P. (1974). A patient by any other name . . . : Clinician group difference in labeling bias. *Journal of Consulting and Clinical Psychology, 42,* 4–9.

Leaf, Philip J., Myers, Jerome K., & McEvoy, Lawrence T. (1991). Procedures used in the Epidemiologic Catchment Area Study. In Lee N. Robins & Darrel A. Regier (Eds.), *Psychiatric disorders in America: The Epidemiologic Catchment Area Study* (pp. 11–32). New York: The Free Press.

Leary, Timothy. (1957). *Interpersonal diagnosis of personality. A functional theory and methodology for personality evaluation.* New York: Ronald Press.

Leigh, Hoyle, Price, Lawrence, Ciarcia, James, & Mirassou, Marlene M. (1982). DSM-III and consultation-liaison psychiatry: Toward a comprehensive medical model of the patient. *General Hospital Psychiatry, 4,* 283–289.

Lerman, Hannah. (1986). *A mote in Freud's eye: From psychoanalysis to the psychology of women.* New York: Springer.

Lerman, Hannah. (1989). *Theoretical and practical implications of the post-traumatic stress disorder diagnosis for women.* Paper presented at the Convention of the American Psychological Association, New Orleans, LA.

Lerman, Hannah. (1990). *Sexual intimacies between psychotherapists and patients: An annotated bibliography of mental health, legal and public media literature and relevant legal cases.* Phoenix, AZ: Division of Psychotherapy of the American Psychological Association.

Lewine, Richard, Burbach, Daniel, & Meltzer, Herbert Y. (1984). Effect of diagnostic criteria on the ratio of male to female schizophrenic patients. *American Journal of Psychiatry, 141,* 84–87.

Lief, Alfred. (Ed.). (1948). *The commonsense psychiatry of Dr. Adolf Meyer: Fifty-two selected papers, with biographical narrative.* New York: McGraw-Hill.

Light, Donald Jr. (1980). *Becoming psychiatrists: The professional transformation of self.* New York: Norton.

Lindsay, D. Stephen. (1995). Beyond backlash: Comments on Enns, McNeilly, Corkery and Gilbert. *The Counseling Psychologist, 23*(2), 280–289.

Linton, Ralph. (1956). *Culture and mental disorders.* Springfield, IL: Charles C Thomas.

Livesley, W. John, Schroeder, Marsha L., Jackson, Douglas N., & Jang, Kerry L. (1994). Categorical distinctions in the study of personality disorder: Implications for classification. *Journal of Abnormal Psychology, 103,* 6–17.

Loftus, Elizabeth F., Milo, Elizabeth M., & Paddock, John R. (1995). The accidental executioner: Why psychotherapy must be informed by science. *The Counseling Psychologist, 23*(2), 300–309.

Loring, Marti, & Powell, Brian. (1988). Gender, race and DSM-III: A study of the objectivity of psychiatric diagnostic behavior. *Journal of Health and Social Behavior, 29,* 1–22.

Lunbeck, Elizabeth. (1987). "A new generation of women": Progressive psychiatrists and the hypersexual female. *Feminist Studies, 13,* 513–543.

Maj, Mario (1984). Evolution of the American concept of schizoaffective psychosis. *Neuropsychobiology, 11,* 7–13.

Mallinckrodt, Brent, McCreary, Beverly A., & Robertson, Anne K. (1995). Co-occurrence of eating disorders and incest: The role of attachment, family environment, and social competencies. *Journal of Counseling Psychology, 42*(2), 178–186.

Malyon, Alan K. (1986, July). Division 44 task force on diagnostic concerns succeeds. *Division 44 Newsletter, 2*(2), 1.

Maser, Jack D., Kaelber, Charles, & Weise, Richard E. (1991). International use and attitudes toward DSM-III and DSM-III-R: Growing consensus in psychiatric classification. *Journal of Abnormal Psychology, 100*(3), 271–279.

Masson, Jeffery. (1984). *The assault on truth: Freud's suppression of the seduction theory.* New York: Farrar, Straus and Giroux.

Masters, William H., & Johnson, Virginia E. (1970). *Human sexual inadequacy.* Boston: Little, Brown.

May, James V., Abbot, E. Stanley, Campbell, C. Macfie, Treadway, Walter L., Cheney, C. O., Williams, Franwood E., Hutchings, Richard H., Barrett, Albert M., Shanahan, William T., & Hincks, Clarence M. (1934). Report on the Committee of Statistics to the Council of the American Psychiatric Association. *American Journal of Insanity, 91,* Book I, 433–437.

McCrae, Robert R., & John, Oliver P. (1992). An introduction to the Five-Factors model and its applications. *Journal of Personality, 60,* 175–215.

McGorry, Patrick D., Mihalopoulos, Cathy, Henry, Lisa, Dakis, Jenepher, Jackson, Henry J., Flaum, Michael, Harrigan, Susan, McKenzie, Dean, Kulkarni, Jayashri, & Karoly, Robert. (1995). Spurious precision: Procedural validity of diagnostic assessment in psychotic disorders. *American Journal of Psychiatry, 152*(2), 220–223.

McGrath, Ellen, Keita, Gwendolyn Puryear, Strickland, Bonnie R., & Russo, Nancy Felipe. (Eds.) (1990). *Women and depression: Risk factors and treatment issues.* Washington, DC: American Psychological Association.

McReynolds, Paul. (1989). Diagnosis and clinical assessment: Current status and issues. *Annual Review of Psychology, 40,* 83–108.

Mellsop, Graham, Varghese, Frank, Joshua, Stephen, & Hicks, Anthony. (1982). The reliability of Axis-II of DSM-III. *American Journal of Psychiatry, 10,* 1360–1361.

Meyer, Adolf. (1948). The psychobiological point of view. In Alfred Lief (Ed.), *The commonsense psychiatry of Dr. Adolf Meyer* (pp. 590–606). New York: McGraw-Hill. (Original work published 1934)

Mezzich, Juan E. (1979). Patterns and issues in multiaxial psychiatric diagnosis. *Psychological Medicine, 9,* 125–137.

Mezzich, Juan E., Fabrega, Horacio Jr., & Kleinman, Arthur. (1992). Cultural validity and DSM-IV. *Journal of Nervous and Mental Disease, 180,* 4.

Mezzich, Juan E., Fabrega, Horacio Jr., Mezzich, Ada C., & Coffman, Gerald A. (1985). International experience with DSM-III. *Journal of Nervous and Mental Disease, 173*(12), 738–741.

Mezzich, Juan E., & von Cranach, Michael. (1988). Foreword. In Juan E. Mezzich & Michael von Cranach (Eds.), *International classification in psychiatry: Unity and diversity* (pp. xiii–xvii). New York: Cambridge University Press.

Middlebrook, Diane Wood. (1991). *Anne Sexton: A biography.* Boston: Houghton Mifflin.

Millett, Kate. (1990). *The Loony-bin trap.* New York: Simon and Schuster.

Moldin, Steven O., Rice, John P., Erlenmeyer-Kimling, L., & Squires-Wheeler, Elizabeth. (1994). Latent structure of DSM-III-R Axis II psychopathology in a normal sample. *Journal of Abnormal Psychology, 103*, 259–266.

Morrison, Eileen, Fisher, Lucille Y., Wilson, Holly Skodol, & Underwood, Patricia. (1985). NSGAE: Nursing adaptation evaluation. *Journal of Psychosocial Nursing, 23*(8), 10–13.

Morrison, James. (1989). Childhood sexual histories of women with somatization disorder. *American Journal of Psychiatry, 146*(2), 239–241.

Morey, Leslie C. (1987). The Foulds hierarchy of personal illness: A review of recent research. *Comprehensive Psychiatry, 28*(2), 159–168.

Moses, Rafael. (1978). Adult psychic trauma: The question of early predisposition and some detailed mechanisms. *International Journal of Psycho-Analysis, 54*, 353–363.

Movahedi, Siamak. (1975). Loading the dice in favor of madness. *Journal of Health and Social Behavior, 16*, 192–197.

Murphy, Jane M. (1978). The recognition of psychosis in non-Western societies. In Robert L. Spitzer & Donald F. Klein (Eds.), *Critical Issues in Psychiatric Diagnosis* (pp. 1–13). New York: Raven Press.

North, Carol S., Ryall, Jo-Ellyn M., Ricci, Daniel A., and Wetzel, Richard D. (1993). *Multiple personalities, multiple disorders: Psychiatric classification and media influence.* New York: Oxford University Press.

North American Nursing Diagnosis Association. (1994). *NANDA nursing diagnoses: Definitions and classifications 1995–1996.* Philadelphia: NANDA.

Nunnally, Jim C. (1975). Classification in psychology: Purposes and methods. In Theodore Blau, Mortimer Brown, Arthur Centor, Martin M. Katz, Maurice Lorr, & J. R. Newbrough (Eds.), *Report of the Ad hoc Task Force on Behavioral Classification. I Classification: The State of the Science; II The State of the Art in Application* (pp. 15–30). Washington, DC: American Psychological Association.

Offer, Daniel, & Sabshin, Melvin. (1974). *Normality: Theoretical and clinical concepts of mental health* (rev. ed.). New York: Basic Books.

Olfson, Mark, & Pincus, Harold Alan. (1994). Outpatient psychotherapy in the United States, I: Volume, costs and user characteristics. *American Journal of Psychiatry, 151*(9), 1281–1294.

Orton, Samuel T. (1919). On the classification of nervous and mental diseases. *Transactions of the American Medico-Psychological Association, 26,* 399–417.

Ottosson, J. O., & Perris, C. (1973). Multidimensional classification of mental disorders. *Psychological Medicine, 3,* 238–243.

Pantony, Kaye-Lee, & Caplan, Paula J. (1991). Delusional dominating personality disorder: A modest proposal for identifying some consequences of rigid masculine socialization. *Canadian Psychology, 32,* 120–133.

Pavkov, Thomas W., Lewis, Dan A., and Lyons, John S. (1989). Psychiatric diagnoses and racial bias: An empirical investigation. *Professional Psychology: Research and Practice, 20,* 364–368.

Pitts, Claudia. (1995, November). *Women, psychotherapy and medication: A perspective on the advent of managed care.* Paper presented at the Advanced Feminist Therapy Institute, Albuquerque, NM.

Prather, Jane, & Fidell, Linda S. (1975). Sex differences in the content and style of medical advertisements. *Social Science and Medicine, 9,* 23–26.

Pull, Charles B., Pull, M. C., and Pichot, Pierre. (1988). The French approach to psychiatric classification. In Juan E. Mezzich & Michael von Cranach (Eds.), *International classification in psychiatry: Unity and diversity* (pp. 37–47). New York: Cambridge University Press.

Putnam, Frank W., Guroff, Juliet J., Silberman, Edward K., Barban, Lisa, & Post, Robert M. (1986). The clinical phenomenology of multiple personality disorder: Review of 100 recent cases. *Journal of Clinical Psychiatry, 47*(6), 285–293.

Randall, Elizabeth J., Josephson, Allan M., Chowanec, Gregory, & Thyer, Bruce A. (1994). The reported prevalence of physical and sexual abuse among a sample of children and adolescents at a public psychiatric hospital. *Journal of Traumatic Stress, 7*(4), 713–718.

Reiss. David. (1996). Foreword. In Florence W. Kaslow (Ed.), *Handbook of relational diagnosis and dysfunctional family patterns* (pp. ix–xv). New York: John Wiley & Sons.

Ricci, James V. (1945). *One hundred years of gynaecology: 1800–1900.* Philadelphia: The Blakiston Company.

Rieder, Ronald O. (1974). The origins of our confusion about schizophrenia. *Psychiatry, 37*, 197–208.

Ring, N., Tantam, D., Montague, L., Newby, D., Black, D., & Morris, J. (1991). Gender differences in the incidence of definite schizophrenia and atypical psychosis—focus on negative symptoms of schizophrenia. *Acta Psychiatrica Scandinavica, 84*, 489–496.

Robins, Lee N., & Helzer, John E. (1986). Diagnosis and clinical assessment: The current state of psychiatric diagnosis. *Annual Review of Psychology, 37*, 409–432.

Robins, Lee N., Locke, Ben Z., & Regier, Darrel A. (1991). An overview of psychiatric disorders in America. In Lee N. Robins & Darrel A. Regier (Eds.), *Psychiatric disorders in America: The Epidemiologic Catchment Area Study* (pp. 328–366). New York: The Free Press.

Root, Maria P. P. (1992). Reconstructing the impact of trauma on personality. In Laura S. Brown & Mary Ballou (Eds.), *Personality and psychopathology: Feminist reappraisals* (pp. 229–265). New York: Guilford.

Rosenfeld, Alvin A. (1979). Incidence of a history of incest among 18 female psychiatric patients. *American Journal of Psychiatry, 136*(6), 791–795.

Rosenhan, David L. (1973). On being sane in insane places. *Science, 179*, 250–258.

Rosenhan, David L. (1975). The contextual nature of psychiatric diagnosis. *Journal of Abnormal Psychology, 84*, 462–474.

Rosewater, Lynne B. (1985, November 18). A critical statement on the proposed diagnosis of masochistic personality disorder. Presented to the American Psychiatric Association's Work Group to Revise DSM-III, Washington, DC.

Rosewater, Lynne Bravo. (1987). A critical analysis of the proposed self-defeating personality disorder. *Journal of Personality Disorders, 1*, 190–195.

Rothblum, Esther D. (1983). Sex-role stereotypes and depression in women. In Violet Franks & Esther D. Rothblum (Eds.), *The stereotyping of women: Its effects on mental health* (pp. 83–111). New York: Springer.

Rothblum, Esther D. (1990). Women and weight: Fad and fiction. *Journal of Psychology, 124*(1), 5–24.

Rubinow, David R., & Roy-Byrne, Peter. (1984). Premenstrual syndromes: Overview from a methodological perspective. *American Journal of Psychiatry, 141*, 163–172.

Russell, Diana E. H. (1986). *The secret trauma: Incest in the lives of girls and women.* New York: Basic Books.

Russo, Nancy Felipe, & Zierk, Kirstin L. (1992). Abortion, child-bearing and women's well-being. *Professional Psychology: Research and Practice, 23*(4), 269–280.

Rutter, M. (1987). Temperament, personality and personality disorder. *British Journal of Psychiatry, 150,* 443–458.

Salmon, Thomas A., Copp, Owen, May, James V., Abbot, E. Stanley, & Cotton, Henry A. (1917). Report of the Committee on Statistics of the American Medico-Psychological Association. *Transactions of the American Medico-Psychological Association, 24,* 127–133.

Saltman, Vicki, & Solomon, Robert S. (1982). Incest and the multiple personality. *Psychological Reports, 50,* 1127–1141.

Salzinger, Kurt. (1986). Diagnosis: Distinguishing among behaviors. In Theodore Millon & Gerald L. Klerman (Eds.), *Contemporary directions in psychopathology: Toward the DSM-IV* (pp. 115–134). New York: Guilford.

Sarbin, Theodore R. (1990). Toward the obsolescence of the schizophrenia hypothesis. *Journal of Mind and Behavior, 11,* 259–283.

Schoener, Gary Richard, Milgrom, Jeanette Hofstee, Gonsiorek, John C., Luepker, Ellen T., & Conroe, Ray M. (Eds.). (1989). *Psychotherapists' sexual involvement with clients.* Minneapolis, MN: Walk-In Counseling Center.

Schultz, Judith M., & Videbeck, Sheila Dark. (1994). *Manual of psychiatric nursing care plans* (4th ed.). Philadelphia: J. B. Lippincott.

Schur, Edwin M. (1984). *Labeling women deviant: Gender, stigma and social control.* Philadelphia: Temple University Press.

Sexton, Linda Gray. (1994). *Searching for Mercy Street: My journey back to my mother, Anne Sexton.* Boston: Little, Brown.

Sicherman, Barbara. (1977). The uses of a diagnosis: Doctors, patients, and neurasthenia. *Journal of the History of Medicine and Allied Sciences, 32,* 33–54.

Singerman, Burton. (1981). DSM-III: Historical antecedents and present significance. *Journal of Clinical Psychiatry, 42,* 409–410.

Skrabanek, Petr. (1990). Reductionist fallacies in the theory and treatment of mental disorders. *International Journal of Mental Health, 19*(3), 6–18.

Smith, Darrell, & Kraft, William A. (1983). DSM-III: Do psychologists really want an alternative? *American Psychologist, 38,* 777–785.

Soares, Carol A. (1978). Nursing and medical diagnosis: A comparison of variant and essential features. In Norma L. Chaska (Ed.), *The nursing profession: Views through the mist* (pp. 269–278). New York: McGraw-Hill.

Southard E. E. (1918). Recent American classifications of mental diseases. *Transactions of the American Medico-Psychological Association, 25,* 253–271.

Speert, Harold. (1980). *Obstetrics and gynecology in America: A history.* Chicago, IL: American College of Obstetricians and Gynecologists.

Spitzer, Robert L. (1975). On pseudoscience in science, logic in remission and psychiatric diagnosis: A critique of Rosenhan's "On being sane in insane places." *Journal of Abnormal Psychology, 84,* 442–452.

Spitzer, Robert L. (1976). More on pseudoscience in science and the case for psychiatric diagnosis. *Archives of General Psychiatry, 33,* 459–470.

Spitzer, Robert L. (1985, December 30). Defining masochism. *Time,* p. 12.

Spitzer, Robert L., Gibbon, Miriam, Skodol, Andrew E., Williams, Janet B. W., & First, Michael B. (1994). *DSM-IV case book: A learning companion to the Diagnostic and Statistical Manual of Mental Disorders, Fourth Edition.* Washington, DC: American Psychiatric Press.

Spitzer, Robert L., Endicott, Jean, & Robins, Eli. (1978). Research diagnostic criteria. *Archives of General Psychiatry, 35,* 773–782.

Spitzer, Robert L., Williams, Janet B., Kass, Frederic, & Davies, Mark. (1989). National field trial of the DSM-III-R diagnostic criteria for self-defeating personality disorder. *American Journal of Psychiatry, 146,* 1561–1567.

Spitzer, Robert L., & Wilson, Paul T. (1968). An introduction to the American Psychiatric Association's new diagnostic nomenclature for New York state department of mental hygiene personnel. *Psychiatric Quarterly, 42,* 487–503.

Sroufe, L. Alan, & Rutter, Michael. (1984). The domain of developmental psychopathology. *Child Development, 55,* 17–29.

Stefanis, Costas N. (1988). Foreword. In Juan E. Mezzich & Michael von Cranach (Eds.), *International classification in psychiatry: Unity and diversity* (pp. ix–xii). New York: Cambridge University Press.

Steinem, Gloria. (1994). *Moving beyond words.* New York: Simon & Schuster.

Stengel, E. (1959). Classification of mental disorders. *Bulletin of the World Health Organization, 21,* 61–663.

Stieglitz, R. D., Fahndrich, E., & Helmchen, Hanfried. (1988). AMDP in multiaxial classification. In Juan E. Mezzich & Michael von Cranach (Eds.), *International classification in psychiatry: Unity and diversity* (pp. 180–204). New York: Cambridge University Press.

Strober, Michael. (1986). Anorexia nervosa: History and psychological concepts. In Kelly D. Brownell & John P. Foreyt (Eds.), *Handbook of eating disorders: Physiology, psychology and treatment of obesity, anorexia, and bulimia* (pp. 231–246). New York: Basic Books.

Stromgren, Erik. (1988). Scandinavian approaches to psychiatric diagnosis. In Juan E. Mezzich & Michael von Cranach (Eds.), *International classification in psychiatry: Unity and diversity* (pp. 48–54). New York: Cambridge University Press.

Strouse, Jean. (1980). *Alice James: A biography.* Boston: Houghton Mifflin.

Sturdivant, Susan. (1980). *Therapy with women: A feminist philosophy of treatment.* New York: Springer.

Szasz, Thomas S. (1961). *The myth of mental illness: Foundations of a theory of personal conduct.* New York: Dell.

Task Force on Descriptive Behavioral Classification. (1977). *Final report, Phase I.* Washington, DC: American Psychological Association.

Tavris, Carol. (1992). *The mismeasure of women.* New York: Simon and Schuster.

Taylor, C. Barr. (1983). DSM-III and behavioral assessment. *Behavioral Assessment, 5,* 5–14.

Taylor, Robert L. (1990). *Distinguishing psychological from organic disorders: Screening for psychological masquerade.* New York: Springer.

Temerlin, Maurice K. (1968). Suggestion effects in psychiatric diagnosis. *Journal of Nervous and Mental Disease, 147,* 349–353.

Terr, Lenore C. (1983). Chowchilla revisited: The effects of psychic trauma four years after a school-bus kidnapping. *American Journal of Psychiatry, 140,* 1543–1550.

Terr, Lenore C. (1991). Childhood traumas: An outline and overview. *American Journal of Psychiatry, 148,* 10–20.

Thomas, Alexander, & Sillen, Samuel. (1972). *Racism and psychiatry.* New York: Brunner/Mazel.

Thomas, Clayton L. (Ed.). (1993). *Taber's cyclopedic medical dictionary.* Philadelphia: F. A. Davis.

Tiefer, Leonore. (1988). A feminist critique of the sexual dysfunction nomenclature. In Ellen Cole & Esther D. Rothblum (Eds.), *Women and Sex Therapy* (pp. 5–21). New York: Haworth Press.

Torrey, E. F. (1980). *Schizophrenia and civilization.* New York: Jason Aronson.

Townsend, John S. II, & Martin, Julie A. (1983). Whatever happened to neurosis? An overview. *Professional Psychology: Research and Practice, 14,* 323–329.

Trimble, Michael R. (1985). Post-traumatic stress disorder: History of a concept. In Charles R. Figley (Ed.), *Trauma and its wake: The study and treatment of post-traumatic stress disorder* (pp. 5–14). New York: Brunner/Mazel.

Truax, Rhoda. (1952). *The Doctors Jacobi.* Boston: Little, Brown.

Trull, Timothy J., & Sher, Kenneth J. (1994). Relationship between the five-factor model of personality and Axis I disorders in a nonclinical sample. *Journal of Abnormal Psychology, 103,* 350–360.

van der Kolk, Bessel A. (1987). The psychological consequences of overwhelming life experiences. In Bessel A. van der Kolk (Ed.), *Psychological trauma* (pp. 1–30). Washington, DC: American Psychiatric Press.

van der Kolk, Bessel A. (1988). The trauma spectrum: The interaction of biological and social events in the genesis of the trauma response. *Journal of Traumatic Stress, 1*(3), 273–290.

van der Kolk, Bessel A., Greenberg, Mark, Boyd, Helene, & Krystal, John. (1985). Inescapable shock, neurotransmitters, and addiction to trauma: Toward a psychobiology of post-traumatic stress. *Biological Psychiatry, 20,* 314–325.

van der Kolk, Bessel A., & van der Hart, Onno. (1989). Pierre Janet and the breakdown of adaptation in psychological trauma. *American Journal of Psychiatry, 146*(12), 1530–1540.

Veith, Ilza. (1965). *Hysteria: The history of a disease.* Chicago: University of Chicago Press.

von Krafft-Ebing, Richard. (1965). *Psychopathia sexualis.* New York: Stein and Day. (Twelfth edition originally published 1902)

Walker, Edward A., Gelfand, Ann N., Gelfand, Martin D., Koss Mary P., & Katon, Wayne J. (1995). Medical and psychiatric symptoms in female gastroenterology clinic patients with histories of sexual victimization. *General Hospital Psychiatry, 17,* 85–92.

Walker, Lenore E. A. (1985, November 18). Statement on Proposed Diagnosis of Masochistic Personality Disorder. Presented to the American Psychiatric Association's Work Group to Revise DSM-III, Washington, DC.

Walker, Lenore E. A. (1986, January). Masochistic personality disorder. Take two: A report from the front lines. *F T I Interchange,* 4(1), 1–2.

Walker, Lenore E. A. (1986). *Diagnosis and politics: Abuse disorders.* Paper presented at the convention of the American Psychological Association, Washington, DC.

Walker, Lenore E. A. (1987). Inadequacies of the masochistic personality disorder diagnosis for women. *Journal of Personality Disorders, 1,* 183–189.

Walker, Lenore E. A. (1994). *Abused women and survivor therapy: A practical guide for the psychotherapist.* Washington, DC: American Psychological Association.

Walter, Bruno. (1977). Introduction: Theme and variations. In Rudolf F. Vollman (Ed.), *The menstrual cycle* (pp. 1–10). Philadelphia: W. B. Saunders.

Wandrei, Karin E., & Karls, James M. (1994). Structure of the PIE system. In James M. Karls & Karin E. Wandrei (Eds.), *Person-In-Environment system: The PIE classification system for social functioning problems* (pp. 23–40). Washington, DC: NASW Press.

Weissman, Myrna M., & Klerman, Gerald L. (1977). Sex differences and the epidemiology of depression. *Archives of General Psychiatry, 34,* 98–111.

Weissman, Myrna M., & Klerman, Gerald L. (1979). Sex differences and the epidemiology of depression. In Edith S. Gomberg & Violet Franks (Eds.), *Gender and disordered behavior* (pp. 381–425). New York: Brunner/Mazel.

Westermeyer, Jerry F., & Harrow, Martin. (1984). Prognosis and outcome using broad (DSM-II) and narrow (DSM-III) concepts of schizophrenia. *Schizophrenia Bulletin, 10,* 624–637.

Widiger, Thomas A. (1987). The self-defeating personality disorder. *Journal of Personality Disorders, 1,* 157–160.

Widiger, Thomas A. (1993). The DSM-III-R categorical personality disorder diagnoses: A critique and an alternative. *Psychological Inquiry, 4,* 75–90.

Widiger, Thomas A., & Trull, Timothy J. (1991). Diagnosis and clinical assessment. *Annual Review of Psychology, 42,* 109–133.

Widiger, Thomas A., & Trull, Timothy J. (1992). Personality and psychopathology: An application of the five-factors model. *Journal of Personality, 60,* 363–393.

Wig, Narenda N., & Parhee, R. (1988). Acute and transient psychoses: A view from the developing countries. In Juan E. Mezzich & Michael von Cranach (Eds.), *International classification in psychiatry: Unity and diversity* (pp. 115–121). New York: Cambridge University Press.

Williams, Janet B. W., & Wilson, Holly Skodol. (1982). A psychiatric nursing perspective on DSM-III. *Journal of Psychosocial Nursing and Mental Health Services, 20*(4), 14–20.

Wood, Ann Douglas. (1973). "The fashionable diseases": Women's complaints and their treatment in nineteenth-century America. *Journal of Interdisciplinary History, 4*(1), 25–52.

Wood, Julia T. (1995). Feminist scholarship and the study of relationships. *Journal of Social and Personal Relationships, 12*(1), 103–120.

Worrell, Judith, & Etaugh, Claire. (1994). Transforming theory and research with women: Themes and variations. *Psychology of Women Quarterly, 18,* 443–450.

Wyatt, Gail Elizabeth. (1985). The sexual abuse of Afro-American and White-American women in childhood. *Child Abuse and Neglect, 9,* 507–519.

Yeazell, Ruth Bernard. (Ed.). (1981). *The death and life of Alice James.* Berkeley, CA: University of California Press.

Young, Mitchell B., & Erickson, Cassandra A. (1988). Cultural impediments to recovery: PTSD in contemporary America. *Journal of Traumatic Stress, 1*(4), 431–433.

Zimmerman, Mark. (1988). Why are we rushing to publish DSM-IV? *Archives of General Psychiatry, 45,* 1135–1138.

Zusman, Jack. (1973). Some explanations of the changing appearance of psychotic patients: Antecedents of the social breakdown syndrome concept. In Richard H. Price & Bruce Denner (Eds.), *The making of a mental patient* (pp. 280–313). New York: Holt, Rinehart and Winston.

INDEX

Abortion, 66
Abuse disorders, 153
Abusive personality disorder, 29, 31
Acute schizophrenic episode, 42
Acute stress disorder, 51–52, 88
Acute undifferentiated schizophrenia, 41–42
Adjustment disorder: *DSM-I* and, 48; *DSM-III-R* and, 49; *DSM-IV* and, 49; posttraumatic stress disorder and, 48, 49
Adjustment reactions, 26, 39
Adynamias, 16
Affective personality, 38
Africa, classification system in, 128–29
Alcoholic intoxication, *DSM-I* and, 60
Alcoholism, *DSM-II* and, 22, 46
Alienists, 11
Alternative classification systems, 117–32, 155; dimensional diagnosis, 98; from nursing, 117–19, 120–21; in other countries, 127–32; from psychology, 124–27; from social work, 119, 122–24, 151, 155, 156
American Medico-Psychological Association, 18

American Psychiatric Association, 19; clinical usefulness and, 107; Committee on Statistics of, 19; membership of, 74; sexual abuse by therapists and, 83; Standard Nomenclature of Disease of, 19–20, 57
American Psychological Association, *DSM-III* and, 91, 93
Anarchia, 12
Anorexia nervosa, 20, 60. *See also* Eating disorders
Antisocial personality, 25
Anxiety disorders: changes in concept of over time, 53; *DSM-III* and, 25; *DSM-IV* and, 64; women and, 53
Anxiety neurosis: *DSM-II* and, 22; Research Diagnostic Criteria and, 25
Anxiety reaction: *DSM-I* and, 20, 53; *DSM-II* and, 53; in War Department Nomenclature, 20
Anxiety state, Standard Nomenclature of Diseases and, 20
Association of Medical Superintendents of American Institutions for the Insane, 19
Asthenic reaction, 20
Axis, as dimension, 27